The Truth about Guys

One Guy Reveals What Every Girl Should Know

CHAD EASTHAM

THOMAS NELSON
Since 1798

NASHVILLE   DALLAS   MEXICO CITY   RIO DE JANEIRO

Published in Nashville, Tennessee, by Tommy Nelson. Tommy Nelson is a registered trademark of Thomas Nelson, Inc.

Tommy Nelson® titles may be purchased in bulk for educational, business, fund-raising, or sales promotional use. For information, please e-mail SpecialMarkets@ ThomasNelson.com.

Scripture quotations are from the New Century Version®, © 2005 by Thomas Nelson, Inc. All rights reserved.

978-1-4003-1729-5 (2012 edition)

The Library of Congress has cataloged the earlier edition as follows:

Eastham, Chad, 1980-
 The truth about guys : one guy reveals what every girl should know / by Chad Eastham.
     p. cm.
 Includes bibliographical references.
 ISBN: 978-1-4003-0968-9
 1. Man-woman relationships—Religious aspects—Christianity. 2. Teenage boys.
3. Adolescence. I. Title.
 BT705.8.E27 2006
 248.8'3—dc22   2006021279

Printed in the United States of America
11 12 13 14 15 QG 6 5 4 3 2 1

To Ryan, Taylor, and Kyle . . .
Your uncle loves you always.

Probably some of the best advice I've ever
read about the opposite sex:

{ Love each other like brothers
and sisters. Give each other
more honor than you want for
yourselves.

—Romans 12:10 }

To learn even more of the truth about guys while you read, head over to www.thomasnelson.com/truthaboutguys for free streaming of *The Truth About Guys* DVD!

You'll see interviews with teens and recording artist friends captured at conferences and music festivals, as well as Chad's stage presentation on the truth about guys. Learn what they're thinking, why they act the way they do, and how guys and girls can have meaningful, fun relationships without all that unnecessary drama!

CONTENTS

Contents

THE TRUTH ABOUT ME

Some days are terrible. I will always remember a terrible day in June, sitting alone in my dimly lit, padded security room. I was angry and crying after being restrained on the floor, which was cold and smelled bad. I'd been taken to a long-term intensive drug and alcohol treatment facility, right after being in juvenile detention, which was equally fun. I remember thinking, *How did I get here? How did I wind up in some sad, lonely room by myself?* I didn't want to be here. I was supposed to be laughing, trying to impress a cute girl, trying to fit in with normal guys who tell dumb jokes and burp a lot. I was not supposed to be here. But I was not a normal kid. It's funny how when you are young, you want to feel normal, and when you get older, you want to feel unique and different from everyone else. Maybe my timeline was reversed.

Some lousy life circumstances, mixed with my own terrible decisions and insecurities, had led me to this point. The point in the padded room where I was still gagging over the smell. It felt like I had reached the end. It really did. I was ready to give up. And that would have been sad. Because what felt like the end was really just the beginning.

I spent just over a year there. A year playing ball in caged basketball courts, sleeping in stripped-down rooms with locks, and eating meals in total silence. These things make a year feel like a long time—in case you wanted to know. At one point, I was convinced that I was going to get out, and there were going to be flying cars and vending machines that gave you puppies, or something equally futuristic—because that's how long it felt. But when I wasn't thinking about vending-machine puppies, I started looking around and watching people.

I realized something kind of simple, but helpful. I wasn't the only person who wanted to feel normal and accepted. It was there, in that ugly building with all the screwups like me, that it dawned on me that people didn't have everything figured out. In fact, a lot of people had practically nothing figured out from what I could tell—myself included. It didn't matter where we came from; all of us longed for something more . . . things like a real friend, someone who believed in us and thought we were pretty great, and a life that made sense.

I wish that people would have just talked to me back then in a way that I could understand. I thought I was dumb and just couldn't get it. I wish they would have talked *with* me and not *at* me. I would have listened.

I'll always remember the first time after rehab that I was sent to talk with other kids at juvenile detention centers. I had been asked to share my experiences with them and encourage them. I had no clue what to say, so I just sat down and asked questions. I realized that quite a lot of them felt hopeless. I told them I used to think I was hopeless too, but I didn't feel that way anymore. And maybe if they held on and opened up, they wouldn't either. Then later, as I spoke at a few camps, churches, high schools, and colleges, I found the same thing to be true. Teens want people to be real with them, to understand them, and to talk with them in a way that makes sense.

Unfortunately, a lot of adults don't give teens much credit. The obvious fact is that teenagers (that's you, probably) need people to talk with them in the language of the world they live in. People did eventually come into my life when I was a teenager and tell me I was important. They talked *with* me, and I listened. It saved my life. I like my living self. So saving my life meant a lot to me. I mean . . . obviously. They told me I was valuable and helped me see some things that might be pretty good about me. Guess what? There are a lot of things that are pretty awesome about every person. Sometimes we just need others to help us see them, or perhaps a stern reminder that we all have a lot of value. We are valuable for hundreds of thousands of reasons. But the most important one is because God made each of us unique. As guys, as girls, as individuals. If we believe this, we can better understand how to relate to one another.

In other words, the more we know about one another, the better off we all are.

That's why I wrote this book, so that in some small way you might better understand yourself, as well as some things about guys. Then hopefully you can learn to make better decisions about how to respond to the guys in your life.

I hope you know that you're valuable, no matter what your life circumstances are or have been. I hope you know that you belong. You fit in. You're normal, and I'm convinced that you should have a life of meaning and purpose. Also, lots of fun.

And I've learned something else about teens. Eventually, you are going to make your own decisions. I mean . . . really, you are. At some point, no one is going to stop you. I hope that you will make good ones. Not because you're supposed to, but because you can. Life has a lot to offer. I hope you'll squeeze all the good you can from it.

Thanks for taking a moment to get to know me. I'm excited for your journey. Like, super-duper excited. Well . . . maybe just excited.

—Chad Eastham

GUYS ARE WEIRD

Since you're reading this book, you may be wondering a few things about guys. Obviously. Why do they do the things they do? What makes guys do stuff that seems so odd and makes no sense to you?

You're not alone. Girls wonder about guys . . . it's just a fact of life. Just like guys wonder about girls. You are built for one another. So how do you find out the truth about guys?

The truth, the whole truth, and nothing but the truth (did I just swear an oath in court?) about guys can't be summed up in a few words. Hey . . . this is important. There is no simple formula with easy answers to all of your questions. There are a lot of people, and no two are the same. But we still look for answers about one another. Especially when your head and heart are probably screaming with millions of questions. Perhaps your questions sound something like this:

- Why do guys try to act tough?
- Why do guys think it's cool to fight?
- Why do guys always do gross stuff?
- Why do guys think and talk about sex so much?
- Why are some guys such jerks?
- Why do guys care so much about what girls look like?
- Why don't guys like to talk about their feelings?
- Why do guys send confusing signals to girls?
- What does a guy really want in a girl?
- Why are guys so different from girls?

While this book won't answer every question you have about guys, it will explore some of the stuff about them that you may not realize. We'll dig deeper into the real whys and why-nots behind the somewhat baffling—and often just plain odd—things that guys do.

> Nobody will ever win the battle of the sexes. There's too much fraternizing with the enemy.
>
> —Henry Kissinger

Don't just sit back and relax. If you want to know the truth about guys, I'd recommend that you ask all of the same questions about *yourself*. 'Cause it's not just about guys; it's about girls too.

And it's *never* about just catching a guy you want, bashing either gender, or changing who you are. None of that works in the long run anyway. I am writing this so that it might help you understand guys better. And perhaps, more important, you'll better understand yourself in relation to them.

I'm not a teenager anymore. I know this because I got kicked out of a Chuck E. Cheese recently. In my defense, I had to use the bathroom really bad, and it was the only place open. Kind of an emergency situation, if you know what I mean. When I walked out of the bathroom, security was waiting for me and escorted me out. They told me that single adult men were not allowed in Chuck E. Cheese. Sooo . . . that was awkward. That's not the only reason I know I'm not fourteen, but it pretty much cemented it for me. But as a non-fourteen-year-old, I can now see the teenage years in a different light. And I can use my own experiences to help make sense of some of the things that you are experiencing as a teen. Over the years I've been a counselor and a camp director, and I've run youth organizations in and out of schools. I really care about what guys and girls go through in their teen years.

Although I'm a guy and you're a girl (I'm guessing since you're reading this book), in the end we have to understand not only ourselves but each other. The more we understand each other, the better off we are when it comes to making things work. If girls understand some basic stuff about guys, it may just make life more manageable and even a whole lot more fun! That's what this book is about.

Let's get started, shall we?

If men and women are to understand each other, to enter into each other's nature with mutual sympathy, and to become capable of genuine comradeship, the foundation must be laid in youth.

—Henry Ellis

Girl Stuff

{ I came to give life—life in all its
fullness.

—John 10:10 }

chapter 1

GIRLS ARE NEATO AND STUFF

{
There is a woman at the beginning
of all great things.

—Alphonse de Lamartine
}

As my friend Kurt walked down the hall of his high school, he turned the corner and headed for his locker. It was hard to miss what had been done. Streamers, balloons, and a huge, glittery sign screamed HAPPY BIRTHDAY from his locker. His girlfriend, Traci, had obviously remembered.

Sure, he felt a little flushed as he fiddled with the lock and felt the stares of the kids around him, but inside he felt pretty good. As he opened the door, even more surprises were waiting. Tickets to the Cubs game were taped to the back of the locker door, and a

large plastic container was filled with homemade choc-
olate chip cookies waiting to be eaten. Excellent. Any
embarrassment that he may have had to deal with from
the decorations had just been offset by the cookies. He
reached in and took a bite.

It's Simple. Guys Like Girls.

I can't recall a recent story about a guy baking cookies at home
just to treat himself. We just don't do that. As much as we love
cookies—I mean, seriously, who hates cookies?—it's not something you see guys doing with their downtime.

Without girls, guys would be a mess! You do all kinds of
things that are sweet, kind, and wonderful. All those girly
traits you have are the missing pieces that complete the puzzle
of a guy's world. Girls are pretty great, and most of the time you
smell better than we do. Congratulations on that.

> Mountains are spectacular because they are mountains.
> There doesn't need to be any explanation for why they
> captivate us. They just do. We look at them in awe.
>
> Girls are even more intriguing than mountains, and
> given how cool mountains are to look at, and how much
> more guys would rather look at girls than mountains,
> that should say something.

So, *girls rule.* Why? For starters . . . you smile prettier
than guys do, and like I said, you smell way better. There are

probably a few hundred other reasons as well. We'll get to a lot of them eventually.

Also, you were born. Congrats on that. That's all it takes. I'm not sure a lot of girls understand this very simple point. You are a girl. Therefore, you are valuable and guys will like you. Promise. Don't argue. Not only are you valuable and interesting to guys, but you are also valuable to God. I like God because he says we are all pretty important, and he decorated this whole planet with hints of this truth: we are valuable. I like it when people say I'm valuable. I like this about God very much, that he keeps telling us how much we mean to him and to one another.

I spend a lot of time trying to understand young people and the things they go through. Through the interactions I have with teens all over the country, I get glimpses into what young people's lives are like.

As much as guys love sports and music, trying to be clever, getting dirty, lighting things on fire, and lifting weights, there is something that will always appeal to guys much more than all of that—YOU! You will. Females. Girls. *You.*

Guys like girls, love girls, need girls, and, as mentioned earlier, guys like the way girls smell. Guys eventually learn that everything is at least balanced, if not better, because of girls.

Things Treasured

Here are just a few things that most guys love about most girls, even if they don't know it or show it:

💎 Girls are dependable.   *continued . . .*

💎 Girls smile, and it's really neat.

💎 Girls' voices are very attractive to guys.

💎 Girls are more aware of words and feelings, even from a young age.

💎 Girls are great listeners.

💎 Girls are often more sensitive than guys.

💎 Girls make us feel strong.

💎 Girls put a lot of effort into everything they do.

💎 Girls are more organized.

💎 Girls are great at multitasking.

GIRLS ARE REALLY COOL

There is something I've observed about girls in the classroom, in youth groups, at football games, at restaurants, walking down the street, pretty much everywhere actually. Girls are really cool. I mean that. You really are. Sure, you're a little silly sometimes, but you're fun and sweet and hilarious. Actually, guys are great too—don't get me wrong. It's just that guys, especially between the ages of thirteen and eighteen, try so hard to be macho. They can't help it. We'll tackle that later.

> Be a friend to thyself, and others will be so too.
> —Thomas Fuller

Now that I'm a bit older, here's what I see: guys and girls are distinctly *different*. God chose to make women unique, and there is nothing else like them in all of his creation. Men have written about women in love poems,

6

novels, poetry, and music throughout time—yet our fascination with women never lessens! Women stir up wonder, amazement, and pure mystery in the very fabric of men. In some small way, we are trying to capture your true nature—a goal that can never fully be realized. Still, we try.

Guys have always been completely and utterly fascinated with the girl creature! If the mountains and oceans are the peaks of God's earthly creation, then women are by far his best creation when it comes to living things.

SHHH!

Here's a little not-so-secret thought: God sees you as his beautiful creation. He's the One who said, "It is not good for the man to be alone" (Genesis 2:18). So he made women. No guy can make you into anything more beautiful than God already has. A guy's job is to affirm the worth you have already been given.

▷ DISCUSSION STUFF ◁

1. What are three of the most confusing questions you have about guys?
2. In what ways are you letting yourself, your value, your worth, be defined by other people?
3. Have you let other people take away some of your value?
4. What are three great things that you wish guys knew about you? (Yes, you have to think of three whole things.)
5. What mistakes have you seen girls make when dealing with the opposite sex?

chapter 2

UNTIL YOU LIKE YOURSELF, WELL . . .

{ I didn't belong as a kid, and that always bothered me. If I'd only known that one day my differentness would be an asset, then my early life would have been much easier.

—Bette Midler }

What's wrong, Jamie?" her mom asked as she came home from school in a huff. Jamie's face was flushed and wore a scowl.

"Wrong? Wrong? Let's see . . . I can't stand my droopy hair. I've gained seven pounds. I don't have anything new to wear, so I look like a dork. I didn't make the cheerleading squad. And now I've got two huge zits on my face! It's no wonder Jimmy Kennedy doesn't like me!"

"Oh, sweetheart," her mom replied. "You're a beautiful girl. If Jimmy doesn't see that, then he doesn't deserve to go out with you."

Jamie looked at her mom and rolled her eyes. "I knew you wouldn't understand," she said.

Guess What

Girls are pretty great in lots of ways. Just in case you still have any doubts—and you might occasionally—glance through this list to remind yourself how great you are:

- ◈ Girls understand beauty and color. You aren't usually fashion blind. You wear stuff that looks great together, including your shoes. Your bedrooms are cute, coordinated, and everything matches. This is utterly baffling to most guys on earth.
- ◈ Girls are often more honest. You aren't afraid to feel things and speak from your heart, and you sometimes learn to trust more easily.
- ◈ Girls have more clothing choices. Girls can wear shirts, pants, dresses, shorts, skirts, and shoes . . . in about 4 million different combinations.
- ◈ Girls often motivate guys to do all sorts of things guys normally wouldn't do—like take a shower, look you right in the eyes when talking to you, write you love songs, buy gifts, remember special occasions, and even try to save the world!
- ◈ Girls are more likely than guys to dance great, and you're often willing to teach others how to do it.

◈ Girls giggle, jump around, and get really excited with each other for no reason. Do you enjoy life more, or does it just seem like it? In other words, you express yourself, and it's great.

◈ Girls usually observe the smaller things and the details that make everyday life feel more special.

SHHH!

Here's a secret: the more comfortable you are with yourself, the more comfortable you are with others. I'll probably say this over and over again, but it's because it really is important. The more comfortable you are with yourself, the more comfortable you are with others.

We can talk about lots of reasons why girls are great. But the individual, unique you God created may be tall, short, thin, or heavy; pearl, oval, boxy, or pencil-shaped; brunette, blonde, or redheaded; Asian, African, Caucasian, or a tiny little alien. You might be outgoing, shy, an ace student, or one who has to study twice as much as your friends. You may be a super athlete or a klutz. You get the idea.

None of that, or anything else, really matters until you are comfortable with yourself—the *you* God made you to be. A verse in the Bible, Psalm 139:14, says that God made you in "an amazing and wonderful way." You can trust this or not. But really, and let's be honest, it's pretty encouraging and there's absolutely no downside to it.

I hope you know—or at least will learn to know—that you are pretty great. That you are good, funny, smart, kind, goofy, smiley, silly, mysterious, passionate, creative, and a lot of other things that make you . . . you. Seeing yourself as God sees you will help others, including guys, see how wonderful you are!

Maybe this sounds a little trite, like something you would expect to hear from your mom and dad. You can circle the globe for answers, but the only way that you can become comfortable with yourself is by trusting that what God says about you in his Word is true. Nothing in this book matters as much as that.

Guys like girls who know they are valuable. That doesn't mean stuck-up, trendy, or sexy, but *valuable*.

Girls with a poor self-image usually *don't* end up living happily ever after. I wish they did, but I wouldn't bet on it. Sure, sometimes things happen and life turns out great. God can show love, redemption, forgiveness, and real value through our friendships and relationships. But God already made each one of you unique and beautiful. It's up to you to embrace who you are and to love yourselves so that your inner being can shine through to others. That's what makes you lovable—knowing that you are, in fact, loved already.

> You made my whole being; you formed me in my mother's body. I praise you because you made me in an amazing and wonderful way.
> —Psalm 139:13-14

LOOK IN THE MIRROR

The starting point in all of this is *you*! The God of the entire universe created *you*. You are *his*. He loves you just the way you are. Do you see yourself the way he sees you? The Bible says God doesn't look at your outward appearance; he looks at your heart (1 Samuel 16:7). That means what you think is more important to God than what you look like.

> When we seek to discover the best in others, we somehow bring out the best in ourselves.
> —William Arthur Ward

The fact is . . . what you think of yourself will determine everything else about how others see and think of you. When you are comfortable on the inside, it changes everything about how you look and relate to others. This includes smelly boys.

Here are a few questions to get you thinking about where your starting point is:

- What do people think of you when they meet you? Do they think you care about them?
- What are the three best things about you? How would you rank your beauty, intelligence, and humor from one (being bad) to ten (being great)?
- Are you awesome, cool, and fun to hang out with? Are you more of a flirt or a friend? Are you confident or just faking it? Are you selfish and self-centered, or are other guys and girls important to you?

- What does a guy have to do to earn your attention? Is it easy or difficult for others to get your attention?
- What are the three most important things in your life? What are some of your greatest achievements? What do you feel most comfortable with about yourself?
- Do you allow yourself to be loved the way God says you are to be loved?

If you don't know the answers to most of these questions, that's okay. But . . . you have work to do. And like most other girls, you really do have a lot to learn about yourself.

Guys tend to be more enthralled by and excited about girls who are secure in their own worth. Guys can't create your value; we can only appreciate it. You have to be the starting point. You have to know that God loves you, or you can't love yourself—and nobody else can love you either. And the cool thing is that you don't have to guess about whether or not God loves you. (See Psalm 59:17, John 3:16, John 16:27, Colossians 3:12, and 1 Thessalonians 1:4.)

Everyone has value and beauty. In fact, they have it all over the place. It's up to you whether or not you choose to see it. Your choice.

GUY TIP

If you want to know what you can do for guys, you can start by focusing on yourself. How you look, how much you weigh, or how much attention you get from us—try putting all that on the back burner for a bit. Even if you think of it as an experiment; just try. Experiments are fun, right? I might have lost an eyebrow in an experiment once, but it was still fun.

When you discover who you are, guys are free to discover you too. (But, like . . . keep your pants on with that one and don't take my writing out of context.) When you realize just how great you are, then guys will too. The truth is guys really want you to be great. It makes them want to be great too.

▷ DISCUSSION STUFF ◁

1. What are three things that you struggle with that distort your view of yourself?
2. What are five things that other people say are great about you? Seriously . . . they are there . . . think about it.
3. Are there any "weird" things about you (circumstances, habits, looks, quirks, personality traits) that could actually be viewed as strengths?
4. What are five things about girls that are necessary for the world that guys are typically not able to do as well?
5. Which of your traits do you wish were more appreciated by your friends? By guys?
6. What things about yourself make you feel awkward? Do you think that affects the way other people see you?
7. What three traits do you think guys your age value the most in girls? Are these truly the most valuable things? Do you think this will change in the next five years? If so, how?
8. Think of your favorite people. What are the qualities you love about them? How do these qualities affect your view of them?

chapter 3

NOODLES AND BOXES

She said, 'Hi, Kristi. Good to see ya.' But I don't like the way she said it, 'cause I don't think she actually meant it, ya know? The sound of her voice was the same way that Julie talks in class, and Julie said I was getting fat last month behind my back to Josh, who likes me. And I know she did. Besides, who is she to be saying that in the first place? Plus she never shuts up, and she's always talking about herself and sticking her chest out and flirting with people, including my boyfriend, Mark. And don't even get me started about Mark, because what's his deal anyway? I could smack him for acting like he totally doesn't know she is trying to flirt with him, 'cause you know he does. I saw him laughing when she was talking to him in the hallway, and it made me mad because she was wearing the same skirt I had just bought. And he said something about it to her, and he never even noticed it when I wore it."

Over 99.9 percent of guys respond to that with: "What?"

Waffles and Noodles

Some guys were over at my place one night, and there was lots of yelling: "Hit him! Beat him! Make him bleed!"

Don't worry. It was on the television. We were watching a huge title fight for the middleweight boxing championship of the world. And just so you know, we didn't use fancy plates, none of us smelled good, and no one thought to tell anyone to bring something "fun" to eat. On top of that, absolutely nobody was getting their hair braided. We were eating, laughing, and yelling at a television screen as though the boxers in the ring could hear us. I'm sure my neighbors heard us.

When guys, dudes, boys, whatever . . . get together, we pretty much get pizza. It's easy, and we don't have to do anything except walk to the door, hand over some money, put down the box, pick up food with our hands, and shove it into our mouths. Sometimes forgetting to see if it will burn our mouths before we shove it in there.

Well, you get the idea. It was quite the "dude-bro" evening. But as I sat there, I noticed how the guys were talking with each other. Something just kind of "clicked" to me. Somewhere I'd heard that even the nouns and verbs people use can show whether or not they have a male or female brain. And sure enough, not one time did any of the guys begin a sentence with,

"I feel . . ." We were all spouting opinionated statements, starting each one with, "I think . . ."

Listen to your mom, sister, or girlfriends talk, and you'll hear something like, "I feel bored. Let's go to the mall." Now observe guys. Your dad, brothers, or any other males. You'll hear something like, "I think that was a great show," or "I think that's the dumbest thing I've ever seen."

The simple observation is, guys most often talk about what they *think*, and girls mostly talk about what they *feel*.

"Why?" you ask? One way to think of it is like this: guys' brains work like all those little boxes on a waffle, and girls are pretty much spaghetti heads—a mixture of heartfelt, emotional, and squiggly noodles capable of going this way and that in the course of one single sentence.

I'm going to say this slowly and loudly. Well, I'll try to say it loudly—this is a book, after all. It's incredibly important to understand how and why we're different. For one example, guys tend to appreciate compassion in girls more than any other trait. Girls tend to appreciate guys' strength, dependability, and ability to protect. That's just a start. Now all you have to do is figure out how that balance works.

This is just an analogy—the waffles and spaghetti part—that my friends Bill and Pam Farrel and I wrote about for teens.[1] But I think it can help us make some sense of the gender differences thingy. That's a highly scientific term: gender differences *thingy*.

NOODLE BRAINS

Ladies, a guy's waffle brain is a lot more compartmentalized than yours. We tend to spend more time in the compartments we're good at, rather than the ones we are horrible at. And I'm sure that this makes sense to almost anyone.

Take for example . . . getting ready in the morning. If you want to see how guys' and girls' brains function very differently, consider even something as mundane as the morning routine.

Guys make it look simple. Well . . . most of them. Get up, shower (or maybe not shower), eat something. They glance around the room for the cleanest pair of jeans they can find, search for a T-shirt lying around that's hopefully clean, socks if the guy is feeling really classy. (I tend to go straight for the sandals to avoid looking for socks.) They brush their teeth, make their hair look messy on purpose, or just leave it messy, depending on time. If not, no big deal. Some guys do spend more time on how they look. But more often than not, they care less than the average girl about outward appearances.

Most girls I know or hear about, on the other hand, get up much earlier to truly "prepare." After you shower, you spend a lot of time in front of the mirror. Makeup? What's that? I'm a guy. I don't want to pretend to know what's involved in this creative process. Then there's the hair. From what I hear, it's usually not curly enough, not straight enough, not long enough, or not short enough—whatever it is, it's definitely not something enough.

Then girls eat what I would describe as a "bit" of breakfast. Perhaps one-half of a muffin, one-half of a piece of toast, and a glass of feelings and thoughts. I don't think the food items are necessarily accurate here, but it's usually one-half of something, a bite of something, or a taste of something.

Then it's time to get dressed. If you haven't thought things out the night before, you have to consider what kind of day it will be, the weather, who you're going to see, if the boy who's cute will see you that day. Come on . . . admit it. Fine, don't. Whatever. Then you have to decide pants or skirt, shorts or capris, long sleeves or T-shirt, sweater or jacket. Plus, what you look like in each one, if the color works, and if it makes you look slender or frumpy or something like that. There are too many combinations to mention, so let's just say that when you do decide, you're not done! What about shoes? That's another issue I have no idea how to break down categorically.

Wait! Accessories! Am I right? Earrings, necklaces, bracelets, watches, rings, clips, belts, ribbons, bows, and umpteen other things I've missed. Add to that whatever perfume is best for the day's activities, and maybe you're ready to head out the door.

I'm not saying this is true of every girl, and it may not be true of you, but there are a lot of girls out there spending a lot of time in the morning making these really tough, life-altering decisions. Sarcasm. Sorry. And these are the decisions that, for a lot of girls, can determine if they have a great day or a horrible day, whether or not they pay attention in class, and even whether or not they are friendly to other people during the day. I've seriously known girls who wore what they thought was the wrong outfit and, because of this, skipped class! Seriously?

This might be a small way to see how differently guys and girls think about and view our bodies and self-image. It starts with all that noodle-wiring upstairs.

READING BETWEEN THE LINES

If you are a girl, then your wiring is more connected than that of most guys. You don't have the same compartments with walls separating all your life categories in your brain. You are connected.

Girls' brains are filled with little intersections that allow quick movement from one topic to another. Guys like to stay on just one road at a time. Guys like a simple event. Girls can process between one event and another easily. That makes you great at multitasking. Guys aren't as good at keeping track of lots of things simultaneously.

> **GIRLS:** Do your homework, watch television, paint your toenails, look through a magazine, and talk on the phone—all at once.
>
> **GUYS:** Play video games. That's it. Watch a football game. That's it. Read a comic book. That's it. One activity at a time is easier, more natural, and all-consuming.

Doing all the things girls do at once would tend to give most guys a nosebleed. By the way, it's not a fault. It's just how girls work. Girls can include emotional, spiritual, logical, and relational issues all in one conversation. This is confusing to guys, who have trouble jumping from one box in their brains to another. They can end up pretty confused and overwhelmed.

But remember, neither girls nor guys designed themselves or their own brains or how those brains work. If you ever read the first book of the Bible, Genesis, I think it alludes to some of these things pretty clearly. In the story where God creates

Adam, it explains how God sees Adam and basically says, "This isn't going to work. This guy isn't complete by himself. He needs something. Let's see, what is it?" Then God says, "It is not good for the man to be alone" (Genesis 2:18).

And he probably said this in a deep, profound, godly voice. Obviously. And I imagine this was a pretty neat moment.

Go Slow . . . Guys Are Trying

Another really cool thing about girls is how you talk to others. Your brain is connected in many more ways than ours, which makes the way you communicate different from the way guys communicate.

Your ability to converse is pretty cool. I can't always follow what you're saying, but when I can, it's pretty interesting. People's brains are divided into two simple hemispheres, the left and the right. The left side of the brain is logical. The right side is the more emotional side. Each one accounts for many of the differences between girls and guys. When guys talk, it usually involves more of the left hemisphere of the brain. But for girls, both the logical and the emotional sides work together at the same time. This makes most of you more skilled at verbal communication than guys tend to be. Also, girls often have a much better memory about conversations. *"Don't you remember? We talked about that!"* This seems to be said more often by girls than guys. That's because you're better at pairing up words and concepts. And because of that, sometimes it's hard for girls to understand that guys don't approach talking—or life—in the same way you do.

GUY TIPS

- *Be patient.* Go slow with guys. They're usually trying, even if you don't think so. They may just follow more slowly than you want them to.
- *Be understanding.* Don't think guys don't care or aren't trying if they don't talk as much or as fast as you do.
- *Be sensitive.* Guys will do better if you clarify the point than if they have to guess what it is.

DISCUSSION STUFF

1. What are some ways that guys and girls "play" differently? That is, what are the things they do for fun and relaxation?
2. Which word do you use more often: *feel* or *think*? What does this say about the way you process life?
3. List some differences in the way guys and girls your age communicate. How does this affect the way they understand each other?
4. What areas do you want to improve in your communication with guys? Are there specific topics that are more difficult for you to discuss with the opposite sex? Why do you think they are difficult?
5. What does multitasking mean to you? How do you multitask and not even think about it? How might this be different for guys?

chapter 4

MIRROR, MIRROR

{ God hath given you one face, and
you make yourselves another.
—William Shakespeare, *Hamlet* }

Two girls were getting ready to start their first day at a new high school. When the first girl sat down with her counselor, she asked, "What are the kids like at this school?"

The counselor asked, "What were they like where you came from?"

"They were terrible," the girl answered. "They were judgmental and untrustworthy, and they were mean to me!"

"Ah," said the counselor. "You will find them to be

pretty much the same here, I'm afraid." Then he sent her to her first class.

The second girl sat down with the counselor. She asked the counselor the exact same question, and he responded by asking her what the people were like at her old school.

"They were fine," she said. "They were pretty nice to me as long as I was nice to them. I think most kids were fun, thoughtful, and just trying to get by like the rest of us."

The counselor responded, "Excellent. Well, you will find them to be the same way here."

Your Mirror

Like it or not, there is a simple truth in your life: how you view yourself is going to determine how other people view you. Some people say that life is 10 percent what happens to us and 90 percent how we deal with it. When it comes to what you see in the mirror, it's the same way. It really is.

What do you see when you look in the mirror? What do other people see? Do you ever think about this? Write it down? Do you see the capable and happy and full-of-life person that your parents saw when you were a little kid running around, happy and free? Do you see yourself as lovable, beautiful, and someone people want to appreciate? Or do you think all that stuff is just wishful nonsense? Maybe a pipe dream that has no place in the days that you wake up with?

There are these cute little sayings that get thrown around,

like "Beauty comes from the inside." And while these things are actually true, it's not as easy to "feel" these truths as it is to say them. Wouldn't it be nice if simply knowing that truth would help you love yourself more? If it would help take away the worry about how you look? If it would help you know that it doesn't matter so much what other people think about you? I wish sometimes that I really only cared about what God thinks of me. I'll bet my day would be a lot purer and easier if I were concerned only about that.

> Behavior is a mirror in which everyone displays his own image.
> —Johann Wolfgang von Goethe

The fact is, I don't think most teens, especially girls, feel that way or live that way at all.

I was looking through a study one day that really kind of shocked me, made me sad, and stuck with me. Eleven- to seventeen-year-old females were asked about their strongest desires. And do you know what the number one desire was for these girls? I mean, out of everything you could desire in life, with so many possibilities, so many things to choose from, what was it? To be thinner![1]

It wasn't being smarter or more compassionate, getting the opportunity to travel, or being funnier, kinder, more optimistic, or a better listener. Stuff like that just seemed to fall to the wayside on the list. In fact, none of the findings had to do with girls wanting to change anything other than their physical features. For just a second, can I say something? That's really screwed up. And we all know it. But what are we supposed to do about it?

A pebble thrown into a still pond has lasting effects with

the many ripples it creates. And what you do with what you see in the mirror will have dramatic effects on your future. You can wind up in a lot of exciting places and in some really great relationships, but they won't be determined by the clothes you wear, what you weigh, or even the classes you take or the grades you get. I mean . . . I hope your hair is all cutesy and stuff. But the important things, the big things, are going to be decided by what you see when you look in that mirror.

So here's a simple thought to get you started: If you think you're great, so will your friends. Plus, you'll tend to think they're great too. You won't be judging yourself, so you won't need to judge others. If you don't think much of yourself, your friends—whether they're guys or girls—won't either.

{ Look in a mirror and one thing's sure; what we see is not who we are.
—Richard Bach }

Every morning when you wake up and look in the mirror, what you look like to yourself might be the most important reflection you see.

You're probably wondering what that means. I sometimes get wordy and abstract, and I apologize for that. I mean . . . not really. I like words.

CHICK SCHOOLS

I was at an all-girls' school teaching some classes. I say this so you don't think I was just hanging around an all-girls' school, or that I attended it, for that matter. I mean, that would be confusing and weird and whatnot . . . so whatever. I was getting a lot of the same questions about teen relationships, dating, romantic relationships, boys, sex, and so on. I was about to finish up for the day when the girls started asking questions like, "Why do guys just care about what girls look like?" and "Do you know how hard it is to look perfect for guys all the time?" It was at that moment that I realized how difficult it can be for girls, and many of you have a hard time feeling really great about yourselves. And that made me a little bit sad. But I also found it encouraging that girls were trying to understand this and weren't afraid to talk about these struggles.

SHHH!

This is entirely different for guys. We don't try to perfect our exterior as much as girls do. And you know what? We are probably better off for it. We look in the mirror, and we see ourselves—bed head, unshaven, in need of a haircut, whatever. But that's what we see. We don't have the same outer physical struggles that girls do. Or actually I should say it this way: we don't focus on them to the same extent. And this helps.

Stop Looking in My Mirror! It's Not Yours.

Hey . . . cut it out! Stop doing that. You need to look in your mirror, not hers. Who you are on the inside is really much more important than what you see on the outside anyway. You may not feel like it's true, but it is.

There are few things more appealing than a girl who feels comfortable in her own skin. If this is *not* the impression you're getting from the guys you're hanging out with, I'll tell you something that might help: you are probably surrounded by the wrong people.

You might be thinking it's dumb or just unrealistic to say "I am fantastic just the way I am, flaws and all." Well, say it anyway until you believe it. Practice it. It is only when you begin to grasp this concept and embrace the things you really like about yourself that you will begin to understand real beauty. The kind of beauty God gave you. Even if it's not something you always feel, it's a truth you can *know*.

It's hard for me to see how often girls compare themselves to others, from their height and weight to their hair color, complexion, and shoe size. I know this is pretty natural, especially with the onset of hormones during puberty. But when you look at the girl's mirror next to yours, you'll always be looking at a slant . . . so seriously, STOP! You can't see things for what they truly are when you're looking at an angle. Things at angles never look like what they really are.

> To dream of the person you would like to be is to waste the person you are.
> —Some Anonymous Smart Person

Guys like to be around girls who know their own value. Being secure is a very attractive quality. Guys appreciate a girl who knows her worth because then they have an easier time valuing it. It sets the standard. If a guy sees that a girl knows how she wants to be treated, then he usually treats her that way. If she expects a guy to be kind and loving, he will usually do that. It's kind of a self-fulfilling prophecy thing.

In fact, when a girl doesn't feel good about herself, she can, in subtle ways, put pressure on a guy to solve this problem for her. He cannot do this. It will also drive him crazy, and he will run as far from the situation as possible.

Reality to Consider!

What you see is what guys will see.

Faith shapes this subject a lot too. Or a lack of faith. I have found that the times I truly know that I am loved by God, I feel more loved and more capable of showing love to others. And when you know you are valued because God values you, then you become more attractive. The trick is whether or not you can accept this truth about yourself. If you do, and you can embrace it, so will guys. They might not do it within an hour, but they will.

The good news is that it's in your hands. It's up to you to decide your worth. You—not a magazine, not a romance novel, not the attention you are trying to get from what's-his-face, your friends, or even your parents. You have to choose to see that you are valuable before anybody else is going to. As much as that might sound like something I would have laughed at during one time of my life, I can't argue with it. It really is a choice. Regardless of how you feel, you have to get your mind involved.

GUY TIP

A guy picks up pretty fast on whether or not a girl he meets knows she is valuable. And the more valuable you know you are, the more people instinctively see your value.

THIS STUPID "PERFECT BODY" THING

I have gotten to the point that I hate this topic of the perfect body. It's boring, and it standardizes people, and then it just makes me annoyed. The perfect body is not the one you see on TV. It's not the airbrushed version of a supermodel on a magazine cover. It's not six feet tall and 102 pounds with an oversized chest and a tiny waist. There are almost 7 billion people on the planet. There is no perfect type of anything. I'm pretty sure. I'll fact-check that. The sooner we stop accepting stupid and inconvenient lies being sold to us every day, the quicker we will move toward appreciating real beauty. This includes your own.

The perfect body does not jog around in slow motion on the beach all day. That's dumb. Real girls don't stop to pose in the wind so their hair can blow gently in the breeze. Even guys know this much. They may be fascinated by images like these, but they know they are not part of the real world. Well, most guys know this. Some are quicker than others.

The perfect body is not what you see in the mirror; it's the one you are in. And when you learn to love your body, it will love you back.

The perfect body is imperfect. I actually think I grow to love imperfection more and more and to despise the idea of perfection. There is no one single body that will be viewed as "perfect" by even twenty people.

But that's okay. Why? Because you weren't created to be perfect for twenty guys—that's kind of creepy anyway.

Here are some simple suggestions: Turn off the TV. Stop gazing at celebrities. Love yourself. Look in the mirror and laugh at your imperfections. My friend Caitlyn started a pretty cool organization called Love Your Flawz. It is a blatant attempt to both ignore and face all of the messages out there selling us perfection. And you know what? I love that she's doing that. Now, start tossing aside those stupid airbrushed magazines with articles on how to do four hundred sit-ups and have the "perfect body" and say, "Sorry, I couldn't hear your article over the sound of how awesome I am!"

> You must love yourself before you love another. By accepting yourself and fully being what you are ... your simple presence can make others happy.
> —Jane Roberts

Things Treasured

Love yourself, and put more effort into your heart than any other part of you. Then you can see yourself for who you really are—nothing more and nothing less. You are God's perfect and unique design.

NEWS FLASH!

* Eighty percent of ten-year-olds have dieted.[2]
* Studies found that three minutes spent looking at a fashion magazine caused 70 percent of girls to feel depressed, less attractive, guilty, and ashamed.[3]
* One out of four girls suffers from an eating disorder.[4]
* Thirty-two percent of girls, by their first year through college, will have a form of HPV or genital herpes.[5]
* The weight-loss industry brings in 40 billion dollars a year convincing you that you aren't good enough the way you are.[6]
* The average teen girl sees four to six hundred advertisements per day. About one-third of these have a direct message about being beautiful.[7]
* About half of teen girls who are sexually active will contract a sexually transmitted disease.[8]
* In a study of eleven- to seventeen-year-old girls, the number one wish was to be thinner.[9]

You know that you are supposed to like yourself and be comfortable with who you are, but at the same time you're being told every day that you need to be more beautiful and that you aren't good enough. This is crazy, so . . .

Can You Separate Fantasy from Reality?

 Fantasy: You can and should diet and exercise your way to looking like a model, and you have failed somehow if you don't make it.

Fact: Everyone is born with a different body. No one body type is better or worse than another. Models usually have the tall and thin look because of the genes they were born with. Very few people actually look like this.

 Fantasy: Boys only like very thin girls.

Fact: There is no one perfect girl. Every guy is different and is attracted to different types of girls. Some guys are more attracted to petite girls, while others like curvier girls or more athletic girls. Some prefer red hair and blue eyes, some prefer a unique laugh, and some like a girl who loves collecting marbles. Get my point? There are a lot of guys, and they like different things.

Fantasy: Celebrities naturally look fabulous.

Fact: Can we just all agree that this is dumb by now? They are just people. Perhaps nice-looking people, but people. Most anyone with makeup, Photoshop, a personal trainer, a stylist, and some good lighting can look good in a photo. I mean . . . great. Good for them. Can we move on now?

Fantasy: Looking alike, dressing alike, even eating alike is what it takes to fit in well with people.

Fact: Everyone has a different look and body type. And you have to take care of your body in a way that feels

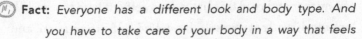

33

comfortable and flattering to you. Being healthy is important, but having friends who accept you for who you are is the ultimate goal. If your friends are pressuring you to be their mirror image, you probably have unhealthy friendships. Sorry.

These are common messages that girls hear every day, and they can often cause girls to confuse fantasy with reality. So be sure you know the facts.

⇢ DISCUSSION STUFF ⇠

1. Look in a mirror for one to two minutes. Write down the positive things you see. Write down the negative. Is there any imbalance between these two?
2. Why are people more drawn to seeing imperfections in themselves?
3. What is keeping you from seeing yourself as a beautiful creation? How could you begin to change your attitude toward yourself?
4. What are some things that you think all guys want in girls? How true are they? Are these true just for your school or your community? Could they be different for other places, or could they be different for individual guys?
5. Wanna do something weird? Okay great! Write down five things that you really like about yourself. Now stand in front of a mirror and read this list to yourself out loud twice while looking directly at yourself. It's called self-affirmation, and

it can be as helpful as it is weird. Give it a whirl. Embrace the
awkward and try something new.

6. What are some ways you think guys hide their true selves and
   their true insecurities? Do they seem more or less like you
   because of this?

7. Do you think guys see you as valuable right away? If not . . .
   why? (Hint: sometimes guys are weirdos and it's not a girl's
   fault either.)

8. Could there be ways in which your perception of yourself is
   pushing people away?

HUMAN MAGNETS

A girl ran into the store to pick up a few items. She headed for the express line, where the clerk was talking on the phone with his back turned to her.

"Excuse me," she said, "I'm in a hurry. Could you check me out, please?"

The clerk turned, looked at her for a moment, smiled, and said, "Not bad."

ATTRACTION

I think a peculiar thing about us as humans is that we always communicate. We can't *not* communicate in life. Even when we are silent, we are communicating that we are silent, and people pick up on that. Now apply that to everything else, including the opposite sex and stuff.

You're always sending out signals, giving messages, or interacting with guys, whether you realize it or not. You can't help this and shouldn't worry that you can't. The real question becomes something more like, do you know what types of signals and messages you are sending? Every girl and guy is like a magnet. They have their own unique force field that can have either a negative or a positive pull toward its center. Do you know which one is stronger in you?

Girls are a lot like magnets. Here are three facts about magnets and girls:

- Magnets attract other magnetic materials.
  - ➔ Girls attract guys.
- Magnets act at a distance.
  - ➔ Guys have always found girls, wherever they are.
- Every magnet is positively or negatively charged.
  - ➔ Every girl has a positive or a negative attraction.

A lot of girls put a ton of effort into attracting guys. That has always confused me. It's like the sun trying to convince everyone that it really is hot and powerful. I mean, it's the sun, it's kind of obvious that it incinerates stuff. A lot of girls are trying to create something they already have.

You were born with an attraction. It won't leave you. You are a girl; therefore, you are attractive to guys. This is probably the most basic statement that cannot be argued with. Sometimes I think it's good to remember you don't have to try so hard to BE attractive. As a girl you have automatically achieved this. Maybe it's better to try and spend more time making sure your attraction will be positive and healthy.

Your desire to feel beautiful does not come solely from looking beautiful. It has to come from somewhere else. You have to realize that you are already physically attractive to guys. You don't have to reinvent the wheel. Okay, so maybe you're not attractive to every guy on the planet. I mean, I actually hope not. Why would you want to be?

When you trust the God of the Bible, and try to understand love and beauty through his Word, eventually you can believe that you are God's manifestation of beauty to guys *already*. Guys have wanted girls since the history of history. We are pulled toward you because you are magnetic to us.

So which one do you have: a positive attraction or a negative one? The question isn't whether guys will be attracted to you, but what type of guys you will attract.

It's Confusing

"Why are guys jerks?"

"He said he loves me, but I never feel it."

"Why does he treat me so good sometimes and so terrible other times?"

"Why do I attract guys who treat me like I'm dirt?"

"Why do guys just want to hook up?"

"Why aren't guys trustworthy?"

Do questions like these sound familiar? I hear girls saying stuff like this—all. of. the. time. They seem so frustrated with the results of the efforts they are putting into relationships. There are good reasons for this.

The four messages that I have gathered from a lot of influential sources for guys boils down to this. If I, as a guy, have . . .

- ◄ freedom,
- ◄ money,
- ◄ my buddies, and
- ◄ hot girls who love me, then . . .

I, the guy, will achieve happiness.

/////////////// **WARNING!** ///////////////

A guy may want to do the right things, but he may just have some really bad habits. A lot of younger guys don't realize that they're being selfish, hurtful, disrespectful, sarcastic, and unromantic. These aren't excuses, just partial explanations. Guys are usually thinking about themselves a lot more than they are thinking about you at this age.

There are lots of guys out there. There are guys who think it's amazing to jump off stuff and fart a lot. There are guys who think it's fun to steal people's food off their plates. There are guys who get a lot of their self-worth from the number of girls who like them and how well they do in sports. There are also guys who think it's great to be a good friend, respect women, and make life an adventure. These guys are not unicorns. I have many friends like this. I promise, they are out there.

Simple thought: In order to have strong muscles, you have to build them. You aren't born with them. You have to exercise them and work for them. And we're

talking about the most important muscle in your body—
your heart. Be careful with it. It's much better to keep it
unbroken than to have to rebuild it from scratch.

//

If you provide a **positive** attraction, the odds for attracting great guys will shift in your favor. There's a greater
likelihood that a guy will want to know you for who you are.
He will work to make you feel more special, build your trust
by being truthful, and encourage you to be everything you
were created to be.

    If you provide a **negative** attraction, the odds shift
against you. It's not a coincidence that a guy might try to get
something from you. He might tell you whatever you want to
hear in order to get what he wants. This may be as simple
as attention or as serious as sex. Even if a guy really wants
another girl, sometimes he's willing to take what he can get
and settle for a girl who gives off a clear signal that she's all
too available. Do not let yourself become that girl.

Sending out a positive attraction to guys won't always be
easy. It may seem as though you are swimming upstream against
the current. Sometimes you'll feel like you just want to quit and
give in to the pressure. Doing what's right, good, and healthy is
almost never easy. If I'm convinced of anything in life thus far,
it's this: good stuff is usually pretty hard. It usually goes against
what everyone else is doing. But . . . it's worth it.

You know what else? You're worth it too.

──────────▷ DISCUSSION STUFF ◁──────────

1. List three things about yourself that attract people to you.

2. Are these the things that people should be attracted to? Why or why not?

3. What things do you do to make yourself feel more attractive? Are any of these things physically or emotionally unhealthy?

4. Do you have an overall positive pull in your life, or negative? How do these look different? If you have a negative pull, why? What can you do to change that?

5. What do you think guys secretly struggle with when it comes to their self-image? Do some of these things show up in the ways guys treat girls?

chapter 6

TREASURES AND TARGETS

Two girls walked into a pizza joint, anxiously awaiting their dates for the evening. One girl was dressed in a low-cut silk shirt and blue jeans that barely covered her hips. Her nails were polished, her hair was beautifully styled, and her makeup was applied to perfection. The other girl wore an oversized white sweatshirt and a pair of old jeans. Her hair was in a ponytail, and she hadn't had time to do much else to her appearance before rushing over to the restaurant after volleyball practice.

The guys showed up, and everyone sat down to talk while they waited for pizza. The girl in the silk shirt clung to her date. She ran her fingers through his hair, touched him a lot, and giggled throughout the meal.

The other girl kept her physical distance from her date. She was just eager to get to know him, but they had a fun conversation.

At the end of the evening, the girl in the silk shirt went off to "talk" more with her date, which pretty much meant a ton of PDA. The other girl suggested to her date that they take a walk through town and keep talking until she had to leave to meet her curfew. And they did just that, smiling often.

THE GREAT TREASURE HUNT

The way you dress, the way you act, and even just your unspoken attitude play important roles in the way guys see you. It's only natural, then, that the way guys see you has a direct relation to the way guys treat you. The way guys treat you can and will affect your future relationships.

Imagine something valuable for a second. Like, really valuable, something worth simply admiring. Does that describe you? Do you ever think about yourself this way? Or would you be better described as someone a guy can take from in order to feel better about himself?

Here is a question that is worth asking yourself. And slowly. "When people look at me, do they see me as a 'treasure,' or do they see me as a 'target'?"

It's not a complicated question. But sometimes the answer can be. Think about when you're spending time with your friends on Saturday night, walking around the mall, going to the movies, or just hanging out wherever. Put yourself in an everyday circumstance that is common to you. Do you feel like people see you as a treasure? Or do they see you as a target? By definition, treasures are something valuable, whereas targets are goals you are trying to attain. It's much the same when it comes to people.

Keep in mind that the important thing here isn't so much the way *you* see yourself in these situations, but the way other people do. Sometimes you've gotta step out of your own shoes and into the shoes of other people in order to see how you're coming across to them.

Most girls—actually every single girl I've ever met—would love to have guys look at them as though they are valuable. A treasured and appreciated human being. I mean, think about it. Treasures are things people value, cherish, adore, and appreciate. And guess what. A lot of guys are searching for a special treasure.

On the other hand, these days, plenty of people are looking for a good target. A lot of people aren't even shy about it. Some are even pretty proud of it. You know what I mean—another self-affirming trophy a guy can brag about. Some guys aren't as interested in a treasure hunt. They are just looking for an easy target. I suggest you not be that target.

SHHH!

What impression do you give to others when you meet them? When you hang out with them? When you date them? Are you a treasure or a target? If you aren't sure, be careful! There's a good chance you might be seen as the one that you don't want to be.

IMPORTANT SMALL POINTS

I know that there are weirdos out there. This is not my first rodeo concerning the strangeness of people. Yes, there are some factors you cannot control about guys. You can do all the healthy things and be a very positive person, and still a strange person might come along and make things all awkward and whatnot. I get that. But most of the time this is not the case. The things we are talking about here are the things that you *can* control, and there are a lot of them. And understanding what you can control greatly improves your chances of having a healthy attraction, while simultaneously keeping away people who don't need to get up in your personal space.

THE HUMAN VALUE MENU

If you had to choose to be either of the following girls, which one would you prefer?

> **GIRL A:** When a guy looks at you, he thinks most guys don't have a chance. Not because you are too beautiful or because you're mean, but because you don't seem interested in tons of guys. A guy sees you and knows it is going to take a lot of effort to develop a friendship with you. He's going to have to use his heart and his head if he's going to have a chance at any type of relationship with you. When a guy makes an effort to meet you, he stares into your eyes as though he is trying to see right into your heart. He's

there to help you, not harm you. He wants you to know you are really important, and he wants the best for you. He compliments you for no reason at all, and he doesn't require something of you at the end of the sentence . . . or the evening. He looks out for you, even when you aren't looking out for yourself. He spends time with you and likes to make you laugh and smile. He wants the best for you, with no strings attached.

GIRL B: A guy looks at you and thinks you are hot. He is enamored with your body. Perhaps he spends most of his time looking at or talking about your face, chest, butt, legs, hair color, or some other physical feature of yours. You look like someone he can try some new stuff with. He knows he doesn't have to marry you in order to get you to do whatever he wants. He's determined to win you over, but the odds are it has to do with his own satisfaction and pleasure. He doesn't really care about meeting your needs—especially not in the long run—as long as you can meet his. He wants something, and he is betting that you'll be the person he can get it from.

You may think those two examples are pretty extreme and fairly radical. And you're right. You may even be thinking, *Sure, Chad. If a guy does exist for Girl A, he doesn't live on this planet.* Or maybe you're just thinking people aren't as black-and-white as either of the examples provided.

Drum roll: finally, here comes the point. Probably anyone using their brain would pick Girl A over B. But if that's true, why do so many girls get the results of Girl B? It's not a coincidence.

Really, it's not. It's you. The thing to note here is that *you* are the person who determines which girl you are seen as. I'll say it again, because it is that important. It's not up to anyone else to make that decision. P.S.: This starts with YOU!

WRITE YOUR OWN INSTRUCTIONS

A girl who displays her sex appeal, a party girl, or a loud-mouthed, insecure girl who is craving a guy's attention all the time probably isn't going to be swept off her feet by Captain Handsome Face who just wants to stare into her eyes all day. Not that you just want to be stared at. That could border on creepy, but you get the point.

By contrast, a girl who doesn't flaunt her body with constant sexual undertones to get attention, one who cares about her reputation and has goals and relationship standards ahead of time, is not going to settle for anything less than someone who cares about her well-being. Quite simply, she is going to do better. She refuses to be seen as a target, so guys don't look at her and think that she is prey. She has those rules written all over her. She has created the instruction manual for them.

Whether or not they realize it, guys see the instructions for girls ahead of time—actually before they get within twenty feet of them—so they know if they want to start out on the girl's terms or not. This all happens quickly and subconsciously. Every girl may *want* to be

> Though we travel the world over to find the beautiful, we must carry it with us or we find it not.
>
> —Ralph Waldo Emerson

seen as valuable, precious, and as someone to be treasured. But in reality, many girls who want to be treasures actually look more like targets; and this is sad. It's even sadder when they can't seem to figure out why.

Here's a weird recipe for heartache: A girl puts forth all the effort, tries incredibly hard to please a guy, thinking the guy will see how much she cares and will love her in return. But reality and evidence suggest that this doesn't bode well. You usually hear comments like, "Why did he say he loved me?" "Why are all guys such jerks?" and "Guys just want sex." That's hurt talking. That's the experience of betrayal, confusion, and pain. What these people are usually saying is "Why didn't someone care about me or think I am valuable?"

GUY TIP

I know this may sting a bit, but the decision about how guys see you is yours. How you are seen is up to you, NOT US. If you know you are valuable, you will be more valuable—to both yourself and others. And notice that I didn't say if you *think* you are valuable. You have to know it. You have to own it. You have to live it. It isn't easy, but most good things aren't. I checked. On the Internet. It took me about nine hours. I got distracted.

Sometimes It's What We Don't See

Here's a strange human thing. If you show a guy everything and tell him everything there is to show and tell right up front, it changes things. And not in a good way. You become an easy catch. Guys like to discover things, so you have to let them discover you. I mean, you like to discover things too, right? So I think you can understand this. Sometimes you have to choose to hit the brakes. I realize that's hard sometimes, because you desire to be known. You want guys to know all about you—the real you. I get that. But the fact is, you can stay real to who you are without giving it all away up front.

If a guy learns too much about you too quickly—your secrets, hopes, dreams, fears, and feelings—he doesn't have much left to wonder about, and he becomes less interested. Treasures aren't left out on the beach for everyone to find. A treasure is something to be sought out. Someone has to map it out, chart the territory, dig for it, and finally discover it. Only after that journey can the treasure truly be appreciated for what it is.

ANIMAL THINGS

Dogs like to chase things. So do guys. Sometimes people say, "It's different today. It's okay for girls to chase guys and ask them out because it's an equal playing field." And every once in a while I hear a love story where that actually worked. But the other 95 percent of the time it doesn't work. Honestly, that's just not the way guys are wired. There's a reason for it too.

Here's why it's weird: If you flirt with guys and run after them, you make them feel good about themselves without them having to do anything. It may boost their egos. They may even be really interested in you because you're making things so easy for them. Eventually, though—and this is the hard part to understand—many guys will lose interest in this game because it just isn't challenging. It's not exciting, enticing, or captivating.

Don't get me wrong. You should always be yourself, whether it means you are outgoing, shy, whatever. I just want you to understand that a girl with some mystery is more attractive. Another benefit is that you don't waste your time pouring everything into guys who aren't meant for you. Maintaining a bit of mystery is a way of protecting your heart. A treasure isn't meant for everyone, just the one who has taken the time and done the work to discover it.

Take Your Heart Off Your Sleeve

Reach over and take your heart off your sleeve and put it back inside where it will be protected. That's where your heart belongs, not outside for everyone to see how it can get beaten up and abused. If you're a drama queen, knock it off. It's unattractive. I realize this is blunt, but sometimes answers really are simple, and this is one of those times. You can still be known and keep important aspects of your heart protected.

> To wear your heart on your sleeve isn't a very good plan; you should wear it inside, where it functions best.
> —Margaret Thatcher

Your heart is delicate. It is your wellspring of life—not a Friday night fun time for someone else. Your heart, oddly enough, is your most important physical and spiritual feature. It's important because it is the key to being vulnerable and real.

I've always found it fascinating that the Bible talks more about the heart than any other part of the body. We are told to guard our hearts. Likewise, there isn't a lot of mystery in a girl who boldly says every single thing she thinks, feels, and experiences the first time a guy meets her.

Lots of girls simply toss their hearts out there for the taking. They yell, scream, cry, and are overly dramatic in public. They're usually either very happy or terribly upset. It's always one or the other, without much balance. When it comes to guys, they are in an emotional heaven or hell. These girls wear their insides on their outsides. To most guys, even if they don't consciously know it, this is very unattractive.

Things Treasured

Remember: you have a heart perfectly designed for you by the Great Designer. Your heart is there for you to take care of. Be careful about who you expose it to, so that it will be cherished and taken care of in return.

▷ DISCUSSION STUFF ◁

---

1. Do you most often look like a treasure or a target?
2. Do you use your outer appearance as a way to draw attention to yourself? Is this the best way to help people see you?
3. If, as I mentioned in the chapter, people are wearing "signs" that tell all kinds of things about them before they ever speak, what are five things your sign says? (This would be a great

exercise to do with friends. Just remember to be careful with your friends' feelings.)

4. Some girls attract really great guys. Why? (And don't even think of using the cop-out answer of "Because they're really pretty." Plenty of pretty girls attract jerks too.)

5. Are there aspects of you or your personality that you need to be more careful with, protective of, or value differently? In other words, do you need to learn to treasure yourself?

Allow your heart to be so wrapped up in God that a guy has to ask for directions to get to it.

chapter 7

WHO'S YOUR DADDY?

{
Before I made you in your mother's
womb, I chose you. Before you
were born, I set you apart.
—Jeremiah 1:5
}

A man came home one evening after a rough day at the office. He was trying to read the newspaper, but his children constantly interrupted him. One child came and asked for money so she could buy ice cream. So he reached into his pocket and gave his daughter the needed coins.

Another child came to him in tears. He had hurt his leg and wanted his daddy to kiss the hurt away.

His eldest son came to him with an algebra problem. Eventually, he was able to help his son find the right answer.

Finally, his youngest child burst into the room, looking for good old Dad. "What do *you* want?" he asked, exasperated.

The girl snuggled up close to her father and said, "Oh, Daddy, I don't want anything. I just want to sit on your lap!"

A Father's Love

You may have the most wonderful dad in the whole world, or you may have never even met him. No matter what your own experiences are with your father, you can read stories about fathers and kids and still feel the kindness and love in them.

And the conclusion that I have come to over the years is this: even though we all have different stories in our lives, when it comes to our families, we all share a common desire. Everyone wants to feel loved by their parents. You could act like you don't, but . . . you do. We all do.

I don't have a lot of memories of my childhood. Most of it wasn't something I want to remember. We moved away from Florida when I was around seven years old. I remember hearing something about the word *divorce*, and it involved Mom and Dad. I wasn't sure exactly what that meant, but I knew it wasn't good, and things were going to be different somehow. It made me angry, but as a kid I didn't know why. I still got to see my dad on holidays and during the summers. He'd come to visit when he could and was always great about it, but we moved pretty far away. I guess it was hard on everyone.

Although my brain has blocked out a lot of the childhood

memories that were hard on me, there are some that will never go away. Most are about my dad. I remember the aboveground pool we had and how my sister and I would ride around on his back while he swam. It's fun to make your parent act like a whale and carry you around. He'd tell us the story of the "Three Little Pigs" and do the wolf's voice by mumbling on top of the water. My sister and I would listen, and the story seemed so real, voices and all.

When my dad got home from work and parked his car in the driveway, I'd stop whatever I was doing, which usually involved dirt, a stick, and insects. I would run and jump into his arms. And I loved it when he picked me up and gave me hugs. Also candy. I guess sometimes we don't need an explanation of how much we're loved. We just need to be hugged.

I used to do this acrobatic trick that I'm sure you're familiar with. I'm actually fairly sure it's plugged into everybody's DNA, because all kids do this. I'd grab my dad's thumbs, and with all my might, I'd climb my way up his legs and onto his chest like I was climbing a mountain. Then, when I got to the top, I'd heave myself backward into a perfect flip and land on my feet. Of course, I knew it wouldn't matter how I landed, because my dad would always

> My dad told me when I went into high school, "It's not what you do when you walk in the door that matters. It's what you do when you walk out." That's when you've made a lasting impression.
>
> —Jim Thorne

keep me upright. Which is better than being dropped on your head.

Perhaps this chapter should have been first. Maybe it should have been the entire book, the more I think about it, because something has become painfully obvious to me. After talking to teens for years, reading, writing, researching, and observing them, it is easy to see something is missing. We are all looking for the type of love that we should get from our fathers. That need is built into us. When we don't have that love, it's like we have to go and find it. And sometimes we don't do this well.

When we aren't loved correctly as children, it usually spills out into our lives, making a mess of stuff. It translates into our self-worth, our self-image, our friendships, our jobs, our relationships, and eventually our marriages and everything else. And in girls especially, it becomes obvious that a lot of you haven't been loved as you should have been.

Multiple Dads

This may be one of the single most important things I know to tell you: you have two fathers, and there isn't a guy you will meet who can be either of them. First, you have a biological dad. (Even if for some unfortunate reason you don't know him, or he isn't the best dad, you still have one.) No other guy on earth can be your dad and replace what you need from him. Other guys don't know how to, nor do they want to.

It's almost impossible to know how to love and appreciate yourself until you know you are loved by your father. If you don't believe me, go and observe the look on a little girl's face after her dad picks her up and tells her that she is special and beautiful and that he is proud of her. Moments like those are when you can see that a father has a direct line straight to his child's heart. Unfortunately, too often the dad you were born with may have failed in his fatherly role. (Even the best fathers aren't perfect.) But don't panic.

The great news is that, in addition to our earthly father, we all have a heavenly Father. Most people today don't equate fatherly love with God. But the God of the Bible is constantly described in terms of fatherhood so that we can understand things about him. Especially the things he wants us to feel. Like protected, loved, looked after, cheered on. You know, all the stuff a great dad would do. It doesn't matter what you've been through or who you are, where you've been or where you're going. Your Father in heaven isn't going anywhere. In fact, the story of God to me is a lot like the story of a father who keeps fighting for his kids to let them know they are loved and cared about, and he keeps fighting and scraping and clawing to make sure they know this, for thousands of years. And that, to me, seems like great news.

One thing I like to tell teens when we're talking about God is this: "You have to know not only *who* you are, but more

> God walks with us. . . . He scoops us up in his arms or simply sits with us in silent strength until we cannot avoid that awesome recognition that yes, even now, he is here.
>
> —Gloria Gaither

important, *whose* you are." If you can't embrace that, you will always be trying to fill a void. Many girls—and perhaps even you—try so hard to find worth, beauty, and confidence in their relationships. And most of the time their efforts fail. That's the trick there. People aren't ultimately the right source. It's like putting a quarter in the gum machine, and the only thing that comes out is a fist that punches you in the face. And then you're like, "What? That was stupid, and it hurt. And I still don't have any gum."

//////////////// **WARNING!** ////////////////

The guy you are dating (or want to date) *cannot* make you complete. If you think he will, you will become disheartened. Guys cannot create a girl's beauty. Guys can't create a girl's worth. So if you are searching for fulfillment in a guy, he will always fail and disappoint you. He will always fall short of your expectations.

///

HEY! YOU ARE BEAUTIFUL!

Girls are usually searching for something. You may be searching for beauty, cute clothes, makeup, the right body, and the perfect guy to go with it all. But it doesn't come from a clothes store, and it certainly doesn't come from a guy. You can try to get it from them or buy it from the store, but you'll be disappointed and hate the product. Beauty doesn't come from these places. It never has and never will. It comes from looking up. It comes from a different source. And it's up to you to see yourself as beautiful. If you want someone else to find you beautiful, this is not an option.

Every girl, actually every person, has a moment in life that's tragic. Maybe it's the first time someone called you ugly, the first time someone took advantage of you, the first time you were neglected, the first time you needed someone and no one was there, or the first time you thought you weren't good enough.

Someone once said that the greatest trick the devil ever pulled was convincing the world he didn't exist. John Eldredge once said, "You cannot win a battle that you will not admit you are in."[1] That battle starts with a lie that says you aren't good enough. Change something. Be better. Look better. Smell better. Act better. Be prettier. Whatever it is, the lie tells us we aren't okay the way we are.

If you're like most girls, you are constantly fighting the idea that you're too big, too small, too round, too thin, too pale, too freckled, too smart, not sexy enough, and definitely not as good as *her*. But God is telling you something different—the truth. He's telling you that you aren't some imperfect mess; that nothing is too big, too small, too round, too thin, too pale, too freckled, too smart, or too not something enough; and

> The beginning of anxiety is the end of faith, and the beginning of true faith is the end of anxiety.
> —George Mueller

that you're definitely just as good as *her!* Your Father wants you to listen to him, sit on his lap, and spend time in his presence. When you do that, you'll find the image of yourself that you're so desperately searching for.

GUY TIP

The best guy in the world cannot give you everything you need. He can't be perfect. He can't fill your voids. Most important, none of that is his job. A guy doesn't want a girl who needs him to be her dad. A guy doesn't want to convince you that you are beautiful. He wants to sit in admiration of a girl's beauty. Affirm it, not create it. But he can't do that unless you let him. And you can't let him until you believe it yourself.

You Are Not Alone

I mean this for real. What would it be like if you didn't worry? Really, what would your life look like? What if, no matter what your circumstances, you believed:

- We don't have to worry, because God has a plan better than our own (Matthew 6:25–33).
- God hears our fervent prayers (James 5:16).
- God knows us more intimately than we know ourselves (Psalm 139:13).
- God cares about our deepest desires (Psalm 37:4).
- God has sympathy for how fragile we are (Hebrews 4:15).
- God longs to be gracious to us (Isaiah 30:18).
- God is happy to give us an entire kingdom (Luke 12:32).

If you could honestly look to God for all these things, you might not worry so much about high school or boyfriends or making out. Think about the guys you know. Then read the list again. Don't guys seem lacking if you believe all of those things? You may just realize that guys are fairly limited in what they can do for you. Guys don't make things; they complete the things God has made. That includes caring for you.

OFF THE RECORD

You have to show people—guys included—who you are and what you are worth. You can't expect others to tell you. Guys don't have the right to do that, and besides, they'll always foul it up.

INTO THE FIRE

It might be helpful to spend some time examining the hurts in your life: your fears, your failures, your disappointments, your heartaches. Write them down on a sheet of paper. Then think about God as your Father. If you are courageous and willing to take a leap of faith, say a prayer and throw them into a fire. You don't have to keep holding on to them. Let God take care of them—and you. God has some big hugs and promises of truth for your life, just waiting for you to embrace them. He's a pretty great Dad, and never stops loving you.

> Because God has made us for himself, our hearts are restless until they rest in him.
> —Saint Augustine

> ⟶ DISCUSSION STUFF ⟵

1. How does your relationship with your father affect your view of guys?

2. Why do you think the God of the Bible is sometimes referred to as Father and other times as more like a dad? Is there a difference?

3. Some girls look to the guys they date for the love, attention, and affection that they should be getting from their dad. Could this be you? How might that get you into difficult situations?

4. What are your expectations for guys? Are they realistic at this stage of life? How do you come up with these expectations?

1 (2) 3 4

Guy Stuff

{ The LORD has told you, human, what is good; he has told you what he wants from you: to do what is right to other people, love being kind to others, and live humbly, obeying your God. }

—Micah 6:8

chapter 8

FIVE QUESTIONS GIRLS ASK

(And How to Answer Them)

GIRL HAIRCUTS

SUSIE: Oh! You got a haircut! It's so cute!

JILL: Really? Do you think so? I wasn't so sure when she gave me the mirror. You don't think it's too simple looking?

SUSIE: No way! It's perfect. I'd love to get my hair cut like that, but my face is too wide. I'm stuck with this stuff. It doesn't do a thing.

JILL: Are you serious? Your face is so adorable. You could easily get it layered—that would make you look so pretty. I was actually going to do that, except I was afraid it would make my neck look longer than it is already.

SUSIE: Come on, Jill. I'd love to have your neck! Anything to take attention away from this two-by-four frame I've got.

JILL: Are you kidding? Girls would kill to have your shoulders. Your clothes just flow on your body. Just look at my arms—see how short they are? If I had your shoulders, I could get clothes to fit me so much easier.

Guy Haircuts

DAVE: Haircut?

SEAN: Mmm . . . yep.

Waffle Boy

Have you ever noticed that guys say things that are . . . well, simpler? Yes, it's true. Our conversations, our behavior, and our brains differ greatly from yours. It's not because guys are simple creatures. Actually, guys are complex, sensitive, deep, and just as interesting, but we are different.

The fact is girls have very different brains than guys. One way to think about it is that your female brain is like a heaping plate of spaghetti noodles, while a guy's brain resembles something that looks more like a waffle![1]

Guys are simply different than you are, and there is nothing you can do to change that. So . . . if you are trying to make us the same, you'll probably want to go ahead and stop that now. Consider the "logical" process that occurs in a guy's mind when he is asked five classic, yet confusing, questions by a member of the more inquisitive gender:

- What are you thinking?
- Do you love me?
- Do I look big in this outfit?
- Do you think she is prettier than I am?
- What would you do if I died?

/////////////// WARNING! ///////////////

Each of these questions is really a potential ticking time bomb. If the guy doesn't answer it properly, the whole thing can explode. Some of these look like simple questions. They are not. Some of them look like multiple choice. They are not. Most guys, however, do not know this. Therefore . . . it's funny. Probably mostly to me.

///

What Are You Thinking?

The perfect answer to this question, of course, would be something like "I'm sorry if I've been preoccupied. I was just thinking about what a warm, wonderful, and beautiful girl you are and what a lucky guy I am to have met you. You make the sun brighter and puppies cuter. Blah blah blah."

Obviously, this statement bears no resemblance whatsoever to what the guy was really thinking at the time. The reality of what he was thinking is more like:

a. Food.
b. Sports.
c. Lasers.
d. Some sort of video game.
e. An itch that needs serious attention.

Do You Love Me?

The correct answer to this question is, presumably, "Yes." If any guy feels the need to elaborate, he may answer, "Why, yes, of course, silly, adorable girl of my affections." Or something like that.

Wrong answers include:

a. Great question.
b. Would it make you feel better if I said yes?
c. What do you mean by "love"?
d. Does it matter?
e. Who, me?

Do I Look Big in This Outfit?

The correct male response to this question is a confident and emphatic "No, of course not." After this, find a way to leave the room quickly.

Wrong answers include:

a. I wouldn't say you look big, but I wouldn't call you tiny either.
b. Compared to what?

c. A little extra weight looks good on you.

d. Lots of people look heavier than you.

e. Big? No. Husky? . . . ummmm.

Do You Think She's Prettier Than I Am?

The "she" in question could be anyone. It could be an ex-girlfriend, a pretty girl passing by, a magazine girl, or an actress in a movie you both just saw. In any case, the correct response is, without any doubt, "No, you are much prettier." This question seems like it has options—and you can try that—but you'll find it really doesn't have that many options. You could always try mumbling something like "Ehhh, she's cute, I guess," but with an air of uninterested uncertainty.

Wrong answers include:

a. Not prettier, just hotter.

b. I don't know how anyone goes about rating such things.

c. Yes, but you have a better personality.

d. Only in the sense that she's taller and thinner and more attractive.

e. Could you repeat the question?

What Would You Do If I Died?

Correct answer: "My love, in the event of your untimely demise, life would cease to have meaning

for me. If that happened, I would hurl myself under the
tires of the first delivery truck that came my way."
   Wrong answers include:

   a. Probably more stuff with my friends, I guess.
   b. I'd give you the best funeral you could ever
      wish for.
   c. How would you die?
   d. Wait . . . are you saying I'd be single?
   e. What kind of question is that?

Here's the point: a lot of guys would be much more comfortable if they just had specific guidelines for understanding and dealing with girls. But because this stuff can't be completely formulated, they can wind up frustrated, confused, and sometimes really overwhelmed.

When people ask questions like these, they're usually looking for something far greater than the face value of the question (as if that weren't enough). They are looking for affirmation that they are valuable—ironically the very thing that people can't get from simple answers from others.

Inside of our guy and girl designs, God gave us very different brains. The girls got the spaghetti-ish, chatty, connected, love for babies, great eye contact, and a thousand other girl-thing brains. Guys got the compartmentalized, one thing at a time is better, simplified and direct, let's-just-blow-it-up, guy-thing brains. We're just different.

Here's the good news: once you understand the differences, it will make your life a lot easier. If you want to understand how guys are wired, first you'll have to step outside of your own skin and try—just try—to look at things through different eyes. It's called empathy, and it's important.

MAY I HAVE A WAFFLE?

First of all, guys don't naturally think that everything has to be connected to everything else. They don't think about girls all the time. Girls don't usually cross guys' minds when they're out on the field at football practice or playing paintball with their friends. At those times, guys are "in the moment." When you see guys playing video games (which they do too much), they're just playing video games. They do this to avoid thinking about homework, stress, hard questions, washing their clothes, whether or not they smell, or you. They are simply playing the game.

A guy's brain has a lot of compartments. Each one is separated from the others. They even have dividers. Guys are free to come and go into each compartment at will. But these compartments don't spend a lot of time together, and they don't usually invite each other over just to talk and connect.

When guys spend a lot of time in one compartment, they get good at whatever that compartment involves. It may be sports, being clever, learning math, flirting, whatever. They focus on what they're good at and ignore the stuff they are bad at. Guys also don't tend to look in the mirror and dwell on their imperfections as much as girls do. They actually do the opposite, which means they tend to look at the features that they like about themselves and then build everything else around that.

A lot of guys find their identity in what they're good at doing; it becomes a calling card of sorts.

In the middle of a phone conversation, guys have often wondered, *What is the point of this conversation? What do I need to do?* Whereas girls can think, *Why does there have to be a point? Why can't we just talk?* Well . . . it's because our brains are so different.

So which one is better: the waffle or the spaghetti? I ask teens this question all the time. The guys very quickly respond, "Guys! Guys rule!" The girls, usually and thankfully, have another response. They tend to think about it for a second, then usually say, "Neither one is better than the other." That's because girls tend to be a bit more fair-minded by nature. And they are right. The answer really is "Neither." And usually the loud roomfuls of smelly guys don't appreciate that answer as much as I'd hoped they would. We all have room to grow.

▷ Discussion Stuff ◁

1. If you could ask a guy anything—and he had to answer you honestly—what questions would you ask him?
2. Do you think that guys want to know about girls as much as girls want to know about guys? Why or why not?
3. If guys really do have waffle brains, does this help you make sense of some things guys do? For example, does this explain certain behaviors, habits, and emotions?
4. Based on the waffles-and-spaghetti analogy, what are some daily activities you do that would be totally different for guys?
5. Are there advantages to having a "spaghetti" brain?
6. Are their advantages to having a "waffle" brain?

chapter 9

WHAT GUYS DON'T SAY

{
True eloquence consists of
saying all that should be said, and
that only.
—François de La Rochefoucauld
}

onnie was trying to prove to his girlfriend that girls talk more than guys. "Look, Emily, here's a study that shows that guys, on average, use only fifteen thousand words a day."

"So?" she said. But she was actually curious to hear the remainder of the study results.

"It also shows that girls, on average, use thirty thousand words a day!"

Emily thought about this for a moment and said, "I'm sure that's the case. After all, girls use twice as many words, because they have to repeat everything they say."

Donnie looked away and then back and said, "Wait, what?"

Something to Talk About

Girls generally use more words to express themselves. For one thing, your vocabularies are more advanced, and you know a lot more about expressing your feelings. Think about it. As we saw back in chapter 3, guys will usually say, "I think . . ." about something. Girls, on the other hand, will be talking about the very same thing, but say, "I feel . . ."

After dinner, Christie told her boyfriend, Mike, "Last night I dreamed that you gave me a diamond necklace for Valentine's Day. What do you think it means?"

"You'll know by tomorrow night," he said. The next night, Mike came over to Christie's with a package and gave it to her. Delighted, she opened it and found a book entitled *The Meaning of Dreams*.

I'll admit there are some regions built into guys' brains where there just isn't much going on. I call them Nothing Boxes, and I love it there. These are the calm, nonverbal, undisturbed portions of the brain that guys retreat to. These usually involve TV, video games, eating, sports, or just sitting around staring at stuff. Guys also have lots of ideas and experiences that we think about, but just don't usually verbalize them in the same way. That doesn't mean we don't experience them. We just have more of an internal response.

Guys don't have the same need to talk, vent, hug one another, and cry in the same capacity as the average girl. And if they did, that would be great, but it just usually doesn't happen like that.

How Brains Work

A study called "Gender and the Brain"[1] mapped the brains of an equal number of guys and girls as they tried to get out of a 3-D virtual maze. On average, the guys got out fifty-four seconds faster than the girls.

"Why?" you may ask. Because guys used the part of their brains that relied on geometry, and girls depended on memorizing landmarks along the way. In other words, for even small tasks, sometimes guys and girls are using completely different parts of the brain. Girls are often better at memorizing things than guys are. You can memorize more words than we can and associate them with other things better than we can.

A girl's brain is also more protective of itself and more aware of what may be harmful or have a negative outcome. You calculate risk more appropriately. That's probably why guys jump out of windows onto trees for YouTube, skateboard off twenty-foot concrete drop-offs, and make little bombs that nearly blow their arms off, all in the name of a laugh or viewer response. Girls just look at them and say, "You guys are dumb. That's dangerous." Guess what? You're usually right. And they usually don't realize it until they're on the ground holding a broken ankle, while their friends are laughing at them. Maybe just my friends. I think they lack that Empathy Box sometimes.

It's the experience, rather than the logic, that tells guys that having bottle-rocket wars with one another isn't the smartest thing to do with our time. It's only after the bottle rocket whizzes toward our face, hits us in the eyeball, and we feel how much it hurts, that we realize it was a pretty dumb thing to do.

Here are a few other interesting things about guys and girls:

- Most little boys are concerned with dominance and are rewarded for being the boss, whether in Little League or on the corner selling lemonade.
- Seventy-five to 93 percent of interruptions in conversation are made by guys.[2]
- Most guys think that becoming a girl would be more restricting.
- Within relationships, girls tend to resolve the day-to-day issues, and guys usually prefer to settle the huge disputes.
- Guys often overestimate their intelligence, and girls tend to underestimate theirs. (Hard to believe, I know.)
- Girls are less likely to be caught and ticketed for speeding than guys.[3]
- When guys perform well at something, they tend to attribute their success to their own skill and intelligence. If they perform badly, they tend to blame it on bad luck or some other factor beyond their control.[4]
- Little girls in groups usually learn to blend in, to be sensitive to one another's feelings, to avoid boasting, and to believe they're punished by exclusion when they are bossy.

Do Guys a Favor

If you want to understand guys better, talk to them in a way that allows them to focus on one thing at a time. If you want to talk about how they feel, ask them direct, open-ended questions. Don't try to read something into what they are trying to say as much. Since guys are generally more direct and use fewer analogies and touchy-feely words, what they say is probably close to what they are thinking.

⊚————————▷ GUY TIP ◁———————⊚

Give guys one task at a time, and they will be more likely to focus on it and do a better job. Trying to think, act, or talk like a girl is uncomfortable for guys, and they aren't likely to be as good at it as you are. Two words about guys' words: *face value*.

Parallel Play

Research done on how kids play gave birth to the idea of "parallel play," which is all about guys feeling more comfortable doing things side by side than they do face-to-face. And it's true. If you have ever observed boys playing at a playground, in the sandbox, building something, eating, or even talking, you'll notice they're much more comfortable if they don't have to look directly at one another while they're doing it. A lot of behavioral therapists say that the best way to talk to a guy is in the car or somewhere where he can avoid constant direct eye contact. Guys do better at passive eye contact. Sorry.

Check it out for yourself. When guys sit in the lunchroom, we are usually sitting side by side, staring at objects or staring into space more than at other guys' faces. Girls are comfortable sitting across from one another or even next to one another, but turned so that they are face-to-face. Most girls don't have a problem with eye contact, even for longer periods of time. In fact, it has the opposite effect it has on guys—it makes them feel more connected. If guys tried to do the same thing as you, they would feel threatened and uncomfortable. As odd as that may sound to you, their behavior shows it to be true, even if they don't know it.

Sometimes I'll walk over to a guy in class and kneel down across from his desk, look him straight in the eye, and say, "Hey, do you just want to look at each other and talk like this for a while?" And then this happens: the guy looks away, his face gets red, and he squirms around and backs up his chair. He looks extremely uncomfortable. His heart rate increases, he feels nervous, and he becomes focused on fleeing the scene.

Think about this the next time you want a guy to open up, talk more about his feelings, and feel relaxed and unthreatened while doing it. Remember that sitting face-to-face, being close up and personal, and having direct eye contact is not nearly as fun and natural for guys as it is for girls. For some guys it can be, but for most it's about as much fun as getting a pedicure and then talking about our feelings and crushes over expensive yogurt—which, by the way, is *not* fun at all.

DISCUSSION STUFF

1. Are there times when you have passed off a guy as "not caring" or just "forgetting," when he may have just had a more internal response? Why do you think that is?
2. Do you think that girls are more cautious by nature? Why or why not?
3. Now that you know some of guys' differences, is there a situation you wish you had handled differently? What would you do differently?
4. Do you multitask? What are some examples? Do you know any guys who multitask?
5. How does "parallel play" affect the dynamics of dating and guy/girl interaction? Is there a way to make your encounters with guys more "balanced" in your styles of interaction?
6. When you approach a guy in conversation, are there things you could do to make it more rewarding to both of you?

chapter 10

IMPOSTORS

> {
> In his private heart no man much
> respects himself.
>
> —Mark Twain
> }

"Hey there," said Jack as he sat beside a beautiful girl on a park bench in front of a duck pond.

"Hi," she answered.

"Something tells me you'd like to have dinner with me tonight," Jack said.

"No thanks. I don't think you're my type."

"Not your type?" he asked with an astonished look. "What type do you like?"

"Someone kind, sensitive, sweet . . . ," she began.

"Then I'm your man! I can be those things," he said, smiling.

"Someone helpful. A good listener. Someone honest . . . ," she continued.

"Outstanding! I can be all those things too!" Jack said.

"And someone who's not willing to suddenly become anything I want him to be."

BLENDING IN

It might be helpful to know this about guys: we are pretty good at blending in wherever we go. We go with the flow so we don't stand out in ways that would make us look like tools. In a sense, guys can be chameleons. That's because it's safer to blend in, and it gives guys time to figure themselves out in the process. Don't be fooled.

Guys don't feel the way we are acting on the outside. Because of that, guys often feel like impostors. But on the inside, where the heart is, there's a lot going on.

When I was growing up, I changed schools about every year or so. Around fifth grade I felt this pressing need to have a seat on the cool train. I mean, it seemed like a pretty important place to be, and everyone was going along with the rules of the train to make sure they got a seat on it. That was about the same time it began to matter what brand of clothes everyone was wearing, along with who was good at sports, who was the smartest, and who was going out with the best-looking girl. In sixth grade I got stuck going to a school in a wealthy area and was put into a class of kids who seemed to all have first-class seats on the cool train.

My family probably didn't have more than a few hundred bucks and an apartment lease to our name. My mom paid the bills and worked a lot, and we got by okay for the most part. But I sure didn't own the really nice shoes. On top of that, I was going through my chubby phase. It was awful. I tried really hard to get on this train everyone was on, but the harder I tried, the more it didn't seem like there was room for me. I wasn't in the inner circle. In fact, I wasn't even on the outer circle.

To say that the other guys were pretty rough on me would be an understatement. And it's not a pleasant statement to start with.

So I spent a lot of time trying to do what most guys do: act like the other guys. I tried not to say anything stupid to let people know that I was clueless about sports teams. I spent so much time trying to fit in that I couldn't really say much about myself, except that I was spending all of my time and effort trying to be like others. That is irony, by the way.

If guys were nice to one another and that was considered a really great and cool thing to do, then your world and our entire world would be a very different place. You would understand guys a lot better. But the reality is that's not the way of this little planet we call home. Teenage guys typically say about nine negative or sarcastic comments for every one positive or encouraging comment. They are in a day-to-day struggle to find their place in the world, just like you. And we are all complicated. I mean . . . people are weird sometimes. Most of the time guys are trying not to screw up and look like idiots. And most of the time they end up doing just that by acting like the guys around them.

Guys usually don't feel free to be themselves. Plus they are usually in a long process of figuring out *who* they want to be. Most girls I interact with are pretty honest about their fears, insecurities, and joys. But guys aren't that way. It's harder for guys to accept that they don't have things figured out. It's even harder to keep all of that stuff bottled up inside.

SHHH!

When teenage guys are alone, they often feel like a phony. A lot of them, anyway. They aren't the confident beings they work so hard at trying to show to others. Guys are afraid that other guys won't like them, or even more, that you won't like them. They're terrified of finding out how girls will react to the real person inside of them. They're confused. Teenage guys are just struggling to get through the day in that circus they call high school.

It's so important for guys to feel like they're included, normal, cool, and confident that they spend a lot of time trying to get people to affirm it. Just know this: if a guy spends lots of time trying to act cool, it's probably because he really is acting. If guys need people to pay attention to them, it's usually because they are unsure of themselves.

We are all—guys and girls—in the same boat; we just don't always know which way we are supposed to row.

JOCK SCHOOLS

I love going to certain types of high schools to talk with and teach teens. I particularly like the big sports schools for guys, the ones where they think football is the epicenter of the universe and that nothing is more important.

When you get guys in a room together away from girls, turn up the truth dial, and start talking about sex and relationships, things get interesting. You can learn a whole lot about the testosterone-driven male. Here are some interesting notes I've taken during my visits to these types of schools:

FUNNY THINGS ABOUT JOCK SCHOOLS

They stink. Really, guys can smell pretty gross. I still get confused about this.

Guys don't willingly talk about love.

There is no hugging whatsoever.

Guys fart and are strangely proud of exceptional gas moments.

Guys are unsure of themselves.

Guys give short answers.

Gay is a common word used to describe a lot of things. It is often more utilized than words like the, and, and it.

Guys are very sensitive and cover it up by being tough or quiet.

In the hall they don't make direct eye contact.

No guy feels like he really understands girls.

Guys are afraid to say things of substance in class for fear of others making fun of them, but they actually like it when someone breaks through the barriers and talks about matters of the heart. Seriously.

Guys don't talk about relationships as much as girls do.
Guys stick their chests out, walk upright, and try to act
tough. Often.
Guys' handwriting is horrible.
One teenage boy to another: "My dad had a long
talk with me about girls last night. He doesn't know
anything about them either."

I love these guys. They are sensitive, inquisitive, and clueless. And they appreciate encouragement and having a fun
discussion about stuff that mat-
ters, if it is done correctly. But
there is something to be said
about these types of schools and
the reason I choose to talk about
them. These guys are a great
example of this reality: guys
have a real struggle between
what they feel inside and the pressure they feel to project a certain image to the world.

> When people are
> free to do as they
> please, they usually
> imitate each other.
> —Eric Hoffer

Don't Believe the Tap Dance

You've got to get it into your head that guys aren't nearly as sure
of themselves as they look. Think about this before you give
them too much credit for it. There is often a big disconnect
between guys and girls. Girls are simply more honest about not

having everything figured out. Guys aren't necessarily lying about stuff. They just don't talk about their uncertainty. And sometimes girls mistake this for thinking guys have things figured out more often than girls do.

SHHH!

I'm going to tell you something awesome. For those of you who think guys know more than you do about life, I'll help you out. And I stumbled upon this little gem of information over years of talking with guys' groups.

About half, maybe more, of the high school guys I've spent time with think they have something very special. That special thing they think they have is a uterus. Yes, a uterus. I'm not joking, and I swear it's true. I usually ask where their uterus is located, and they either don't answer or point to different places on their bodies. Sometimes I say, "Whoa, okay, what guy doesn't know where his uterus is?" And they usually answer defensively and quickly with things like, "I mean, yeah. Of course I do. I thought you were asking something else." Then I tell them what a uterus really is, and they usually get mad for a minute, like I

> Believe me, every man has his secret sorrows which the world knows not.
> —Henry Wadsworth Longfellow

tricked them. Then I tell them to relax and that most guys have no clue and that girls think we are complete idiots for not realizing this basic anatomical difference by now.

So go ahead, give it a whirl. Ask a guy where his uterus is. You'll enjoy yourself. Just be nice about it.

Opening Up

Just like you, guys need encouragement, hope, and affirmation. While we want the world to think we can lift mountains, hit home runs, and fix anything that's broken, we can't. We want to know about you just as much, or more, than you do about us.

To give you an example, here's a letter I received from one very special guy:

Hey Chad,

Today you came and taught my class about guys and girls and sex and stuff. It got me thinking about some stuff.

I used to have a big dating rotation. I didn't understand girls, but I felt better if they told me they liked me. The more girls who would go out with me, the better. Anyway, you said the main reason girls have sex is all about love, but that after sex they just felt guilty. It made me wonder if all these girls doing stuff with me are doing it because they love me and think it will make me love them back? Because I don't. And I sure never thought about them feeling guilty before. It really hit me hard. Recently, I was out with my friends, and I met a girl who was so nice and lots of fun. I loved to be around her. Then my feelings for her grew deeper. I think she might be really special. But she told me that I act too much like a big, tough guy who just uses girls.

I just want to be around her, but I dunno. I guess I'm just nervous to actually have to put myself out there for someone who thinks I'm like that. The fact is that I don't always want to be that way—it's just easier most of the time. Anyway, how do I go about asking her out next time I see her? It sure would be nice to go out with someone I felt that way about. But I'm afraid of "putting my neck out there." What do you think I should do?

Later. Peace,
Mike

> There is much difference between imitating a good man and counterfeiting him.
> —Benjamin Franklin

Nobody likes getting hurt, and guys are scared to death of it! When they fall, they fall hard. Sometimes it's easier to pretend that they don't care as opposed to being vulnerable, especially if they don't know how to be. But behind all this, guys wish that someone would see them for who they really are. And that someone would really appreciate what they see. In this way, guys and girls really are the same.

―――――――――――▷ Discussion Stuff ◁―――――――――――

1. In what ways do you see guys trying to blend in with other guys? Why do you think they are really doing this?
2. How have you tried to blend in with people before? Where do you think this desire comes from and why?
3. Have you ever asked a boy where his uterus is while keeping a straight face? Why not? It's like a free Christmas present.
4. How does family influence the way we present ourselves and carry ourselves? How are identity and self-worth tied to family dynamics?
5. Are there ways that you can change your behavior to more accurately represent who you are? What are they?

chapter 11

GUYS AND COMMITMENT

Kevin and Sarah, a young couple, were sitting on a porch swing. Sarah asked, "Kevin, do you think my eyes are beautiful?"

Kevin answered, "Yep."

After a few moments: "Kevin, do you think my hair looks good?"

Again Kevin answered, "Yep."

After a while: "Would you say that I have a gorgeous figure?"

Once again Kevin answered, "Yep."

"Oh, Kevin," Sarah said. "You say the nicest things."

THE PROBLEM WITH NAKED PEOPLE WHO LISTEN
TO TALKING ANIMALS . . .

I wonder what picture comes to your mind when someone says "Adam and Eve" or "the garden of Eden." You know, the innocent couple who had it all good and then apparently loved apples so much they just couldn't help themselves and ruined the perfect paradise because they listened to snakes and super-liked fruit a lot. Those peeps.

I thought I knew this story. It seemed simple enough. God makes the earth, some mountains, drops in an ocean or four, all in a week's work. Go God! Getting stuff done, right? Then he makes the first man from the dust of the earth. I always thought Adam would be pretty happy and pumped about this whole new thing, but then it turns out that he's lonely.

So after Adam names all the animals, God sends Adam to surgery, takes out a rib, and bam! He gets Eve as his companion. They really dig each other and frolic around the garden of Eden like two naked hippies who have direct access to walking and strolling in paradise with God. Eventually, they eat this forbidden fruit, and suddenly we're all subject to war, murder, jealousy, stealing, insecurity, greed, and cheating. The stuff that separates us from perfection and perfect peace. Thanks a lot!

But one day, I read something that started to change my perception of the Adam and Eve story.[1] It's not when Adam is lonely that God brings him his Eve. Instead, God tells Adam to work. God said, "Why don't you go and name every animal on the planet?" That must have been hard to take. Adam needed a companion, and God told him to be a zookeeper. Did you ever think about how many animals there are on this planet? Good luck finding the leopards, and check out that perfume on those skunks. By the way, lions are big and run fast. Have a good time, Adam, and enjoy the moose poo!

I'm sure Adam was psyched. I'll bet he was wondering why he hadn't thought of it first! He was probably too busy chasing down monkeys. I wonder how long it took him to name all the animals. It was not until Adam finally finished this monumental task that he fell asleep and woke up next to a gorgeous naked woman. He had to have been awestruck. He must have stared at her for days. After looking at baboons for what probably seemed like forever, he was probably just a little more than appreciative. And I'll bet he appreciated her even more because he hadn't gotten what he wanted right away. He had to work and wait.

All this is to say that *you* are Eve. *You* are not to be given to any guy exactly when he wants you. Guys appreciate things exponentially more when they have to earn them or work for them or win them. We value the things we work for.

Things Treasured

Make sure that a guy knows your rules and that you have to be won completely. Choose to believe that you are a treasure, even when you may not feel like one. Uphold your God-given nature of being Eve to Adam. . . . Just stay away from snakes and shiny apples.

A WINNER OR . . . NOT SO MUCH?

So here you are, trying to understand guys. And that's great. Guys evaluate girls, and girls evaluate guys. We size each other up. We try to decide if we want to go on dates or just be friends. We try to figure out why we like to look at each other, come within ten feet of each other, or eventually spend our lifetimes together.

There are great ways to do this, and there are also really terrible ways to do this. So how do you go about it? Do you have good criteria for evaluating guys, and, more important, do your criteria work?

There's a saying I like that goes, "We don't plan to fail. We fail to plan." It's cliché sounding, but I can't argue with it.

When it comes to planning your criteria for evaluating guys, you need to ask yourself if your list is going to turn out well for you, your heart, and your life. Or will it get you hurt, used, beat up emotionally, and resentful? That's why it's important to plan wisely. And sometimes we need a little help to get us started in the right direction.

There are some fairly basic things you should think about when you do this, things that will tell you whether the guy is a winner or . . . not. Run through this list of questions:

1. Where does God factor in for him? How do his faith and morals affect his behavior and relationships?
2. Does he care about being faithful?
3. What's his view on sexual activity of any kind?
4. Is he building a good reputation?
5. Is he showing a balance of many things in life? Friends, school, family, hobbies, sports?
6. Does he show that he has self-control?
7. Is he humble and considerate of others?
8. Is he someone who creates peace or stirs up strife?

9. Is he generous?

10. Is he—and are you—even capable of being in a mature and healthy relationship? Be honest; then reevaluate. Repeat often.

11. Are his pants on and staying that way? Teenage pregnancy is really difficult. FYI.

Do We Size Up?

In moments of honesty, guys know that they don't have a lot figured out. They sit alone at night and doubt themselves, just like you do. They wonder if they'll be good enough . . . good enough to make the team, make the grade, get the job, earn enough money, please their parents, and get the girl. That's important for you to understand, because it may help you comprehend a little more about why they act the way they do.

Why do the guys you know act the way they do? Do you think they're confident about themselves? Do you think they're good enough for a really wonderful girl, or are they taking whatever they can get whenever they can get it? Do they act immature and avoid commitment in their lives?

Girls are usually desperate to know why guys have a harder time committing to things than girls do. I wish there was a perfect or simple or easy answer, but the truth is that all guys are different. Some guys look forward to commitment, and others are terrified of it.

Take me, for example. I come from a broken family. That messes with the way I look at commitment. My parents divorced when I was seven. I have some distant memories of riding my tricycle and running to hug my dad when he pulled up in the driveway after work. I also remember my parents arguing and, after that, my sister, my mom, and I moving away. We moved around a lot, and I went to many different schools. Everything was different.

That experience naturally shaped my opinion about commitment by making me think that it's pretty hard to make a relationship last. Winding up with someone and then not loving each other terrifies me. Even though my parents' divorce had absolutely nothing to do with me, it can't help but affect my view on life and relationships.

Some people have it much better than I did, and plenty have it much worse. All of our opinions and experiences about commitment vary. That's just something you should know. Guys are scared, excited, nervous, lonely, and searching, just like you.

TEST-DRIVE

Here's an interesting thing I do with guys. It's a pretty good example of how they view this whole commitment thing. First, we have to look at the word itself:

com·mit·ment: ke-'mit-ment; Function: noun. a: an agreement or pledge to do something in the future; *especially*: an engagement to assume an obligation at a future date; b: something pledged; c: the state or an instance of being obligated or emotionally impelled < *a commitment to a cause* >.[2]

Now, let's make some sense of this idea. I ask guys to imagine that they are going to take a car for a test-drive. They can pick any type of car they want. What do you think they usually say? Right. Porsche and Ferrari are always the top two picks. Let's go with a Porsche for now.

The guy takes the Porsche out for a test-drive. No obligations. He can drive it wherever and however he wants. It's up to him. He doesn't own it yet; he's just testing it out. There aren't any commitments. How do you think he drives it?

Here's the most common answer: "I'd do everything I could to beat that car within an inch of its life!" I'm paraphrasing, but it usually resembles something like that. He'd drive the car about two hundred miles an hour on the autobahn, quite recklessly, I might add. Then he'd wear the tread off the tires and get about three years of use in a twenty-four-hour period. He'd drive the car recklessly, knowing that he can give it back. Having no obligation to the car makes driving it much more fun.

In a slightly different scenario, things change. This time the guy is buying the Porsche. He has to put down ninety thousand dollars of his own money for it. He's worked extra hard over the last several years, saved his money, and sacrificed his time and other things he wanted, so now he can afford his dream car. He walks into the dealership and selects the interior . . .

The car is his, in his name, and he is responsible for it. How is he going to drive it? Suddenly, guys don't even sound like they're talking about a car. They call it "baby." They give it names. They describe driving it slowly and cautiously. They keep it clean, constantly pamper it, and put the best gas in it. It becomes something precious to them.

Why? What's changed? It's still the same car. The difference is that the guy has made a commitment to it. That changes his entire outlook on the relationship with that car. He knows that he's responsible for the car, so he treats it differently. He treats it with the care that it deserves. And it is kind of strange, because it was the same car with the same value in both scenarios.

Things Treasured

You are like that car. Your heart is the valuable prize a guy must earn, and you are a lot more important than some piece of machinery ever could be.

WHEN ALL ELSE FAILS, READ THE INSTRUCTIONS

Girls and cars are good comparisons for understanding commitment. A guy spends time with you and goes out of his way to think about you. He buys you flowers, tries to be a better listener, and does his best to make you feel special. The guy has to learn how to express his feelings to you, admit his faults, apologize to you, compliment you, learn to say "I love you" and then show that love, and become emotionally vulnerable to you. He has to meet your parents (which can be terrifying) and save up money to buy you an expensive ring.

All of this is part of "saving up," like a guy does when he works toward and selects a car.

One day the guy gets down on one knee with a ring and asks you to marry him, very similar to the decision to finally purchase the car of his dreams. Then he stands at the altar and promises to protect the car, drive it nicely in rain or shine, and never leave it outside in the cold to rust. I mean, he takes his marriage vows. Bottom line, he commits to something he now values remarkably.

This is the time when the guy realizes how precious the gift is to him. So he decides he wants to treat and drive it wonderfully. He wants to do this because now it's not just something he can take back to the dealership.

Don't Let Guys Test-Drive You

You are not a free ride at the car dealership of "test-drive girls." And you should not be given back with a low tank of gas and a beat-up engine. You are a treasure to be earned with time and love. And you are the one who makes all the calls when it comes to how that will happen. Are you going to let guys take you out and test-drive you around to see if they like you or not—just to give you back with wear and tear?

How many times have you heard other girls talk about how sick they are of just giving love? Lots of girls try to love other guys and care about them, just to discover that love isn't being given back in return. Those kinds of relationships leave you with something horrible instead—baggage. Baggage is what you take onto an airplane for your clothes, not the pain you should have to carry around forever in your heart.

GUY TIP

Don't forget, this is up to you. Remember, sometimes curiosity kills the cat. Directions are usually followed one step at a time. Curiosity makes us want to jump from step one to step ten, only to discover we have to go back to step four because things aren't working right. Directions and guidelines are there for us to follow for good reason.

$\longrightarrow$ DISCUSSION STUFF $\longleftarrow$

---

1. Are guys and girls capable of the same types of commitment?
2. Do guys and girls want the same types of commitment? Why or why not?
3. What are three (or nineteen) ways that you haven't been valuing yourself as much as God values you?
4. What tools do you use to evaluate guys? What traits, characteristics, values, and habits do you look for? Are there any that you might want to add? Are there any that you need to get rid of?
5. Let's say that you realize that deep commitment isn't likely or even possible for you and your friends at this time in your life. How does this affect the way you view guys in your life?
6. Are there any sources that you listen to that might be feeding you inaccurate information about your value? If so, what are they? What are they saying? How can you get rid of them?

chapter 12

WHAT GUYS REALLY WANT

{

God evidently does not intend
us all to be rich, or powerful, or
great, but he does intend for us
all to be friends.

—Ralph Waldo Emerson

}

Out of all the friends I had in high school, I can't remember the name of one of the most important ones. She was more of a friend to me than most. I didn't know it at the time. But she sure did set me straight, and I still remember it clearly to this day.

I was in my last year of Spanish class. After three years I could pretty much still only say "*Me llamo* Chad." I also did that thing where I just added *-ado* or *-ido* to most English words. Sorry, Latin-based languages. It was my senior year, and I think it was during a time that I started to get a bit of an ego, mostly about sports and whatnot. In Spanish, we got kind of rowdy, and more often than not, my mouth would start moving and stay that way. That still happens occasionally. Whatever . . . don't judge.

One day at the end of class, we were sitting around on the desks waiting for the bell to ring. I was probably trying to be funny, but it was at the expense of someone else. I don't remember what it was, and it wasn't something horrible, but it wasn't nice either. In other words, I was being an idiot.

Then, out of nowhere, the quiet, pleasant, studious, level-headed band girl in front of me turned around. She wasn't necessarily branded as popular or not popular. She wasn't that standout-ish in any way, now that I think about it. But then she said something that shook my world. Having overheard me tease another kid in class for no particular reason, she turned around and just looked at me. Actually, she looked into my soul from what I recall and said very factually, and with little emotion, the following statement:

"I think that you're a bad person, and when other people meet you, I think they will think you're a bad person too."

Wanna know what I did? I'll tell you. Nothing. I just sat there, and the whole room was completely quiet. She pretty much owned me. Because it was such an honest statement without anger, I couldn't even react or say something smart-alecky. In just a moment, she leveled my entire playing field with truth. I wish I had a picture of my face right then. I looked like an idiot on many levels. Her height was five foot nothing, and she was a giant. She saw right through me. She was telling me I was repulsive and unacceptable. She told me that I was not as cool as I was trying to be. One of the few moments in my life when I haven't been able to speak was right then.

The rest of the day I thought about nothing else. She'd called me out and told me the truth. For a change, I was listening. Even though I tried every way to downplay it, I knew she was right. From then on, I didn't want to be a bad person. I wanted to be more like her, even if I couldn't play a tuba. In a way she was one of the best friends I ever had. And we weren't even friends really. I wish I could remember her name.

"Man, She's Just Really Cool."

Nick is a good friend of mine who is a really lucky guy. He's likable, friendly, smart, and also a decent-looking fellow. Nick has an incredible wife named Anna.

I have always liked Anna. She is a lot of fun when she hangs out with us. It is fun to see how well she and Nick get along. They have a lot of the same passions and interests.

I went over to their place one day when I was in town. Nick and I went inside, and Anna was in the living room reading. Nick said something about cooking, and she laughed in a sweet sort of way—you know, the kind of way that a guy wants to hear from a girl when she is laughing at his jokes. Then Nick and I went upstairs to play some music in his studio. When we got up there, I was curious to know how he felt about being married and having to clean up his clothes and share his food and stuff with a girl every day.

Nick said something in a way I have never forgotten. With

the most honest and malelike sincerity, he said, "Man, she's just really cool. Really cool. It's amazing!"

My brain dialed into this sincere and complex statement. When he said the word *cool*, he didn't mean the word you think he meant. It was a kind of secret version of the word that guys say only to other guys and reserve for the highlight moments of life. It was the way a guy feels when he sees a big explosion, jumps out of a plane, gets a really big scar, summits a huge mountain, or gets the keys to his first car. The use of the word in that way is really rare. Yet here Nick was, saying it about a girl who told him to shower more often for everyone's sake.

Nick was acknowledging that he has an awesome friend in addition to having a wife, and he seemed to think their friendship was kind of the basis for everything. Below the surface of all the guy stuff that goes on, guys really want and need a close friend. We crave it and need these things as much as oxygen. Which is a lot, by the way. We want—and need—a friend.

GIRL FISHING

What do you think guys consider to be the two most desirable traits in a girl? Please guess, it will be fun. Do you think it's your looks? Confidence? Attitude? Maybe you think it's your hair color, chest size, height, or fashion sense. Make a list of all the stuff you think we find desirable, and then put them in order of what you think is the most important.

Obviously, a girl's appearance has something to do with attraction. But your version of the word *attractive* may be too—dare I say?—shallow.

Physical attraction is just the introductory stuff, by the way, and has very little to do with the lasting, relationship-building qualities guys are looking for. But here's the reality. If you spend all your time and effort on physical attraction, you may hook some fish, but they won't stay on the line. That's not what keeps them interested. They'll get bored and start looking at other bait. (Yes, this is a stereotypical fishing analogy.)

NEWS FLASH!

The two key personal ingredients that guys are looking for, more than anything else, are these: intelligence and kindness. Which ranks higher? Kindness. Guys like girls who are kind. The words *sexy, sassy, athletic, tall, short, fashionable, funny, sexual,* and *hot* are usually visual stimuli. If you put words like *hot, sexy,* and *sassy* first in your life . . . you'll miss something. You'll miss being what guys want in the big picture—a kind and compassionate person. When you go fishing for guys, kindness is the best bait you can put on your hook. Also worms—guys like worms too. Well, I do, anyway.

Eye contact is incredibly important. Say you're having dinner with someone you like. Your body is doing all kinds of things your mind doesn't know about but is processing anyway. When the guy thinks the girl is intelligent, funny, and kind, his pupils dilate during the conversation. (That means the little black parts of his eyes become almost twice their normal size!) This sets off chemical reactions that help his body create more chemicals, like oxytocin and vasopressin, which bond people together and make them more attracted to one another. This doesn't happen the same way when a guy is just physically attracted to a girl. It really is the other stuff that attracts guys to you.

If you want to become the real version of attractive, you can't fake it. You might be able to do it for a while, but it will catch up with you. You have to work on the things that really matter. You have to spend more time on your mind, your spirit, your heart, and how you treat other people. These are the things that make guys want you. I know it can seem like boys don't pay attention to those things as much. And sometimes you're right: *boys* don't. But eventually *men* will. And you should start developing those things now. Just don't like men yet. Stick with boys for now. *Creeeepy.*

Here's the best part. If you're spending time on your heart, spirit, and mind, it doesn't matter if this doesn't hook someone into a long-lasting relationship. You'll still make great friends. And remember, you probably don't want to hook an entire school of fish. You just need that someone who will appreciate you for who you really are. You want to see if his pupils get bigger when you smile, laugh, and talk.

FRIEND OR FOE?

I had to write an article for a magazine about the traits that guys look for in girls when they're dating. And let's be honest, I have no interest in trying to speak for all guys on this subject, nor could I. But I gave it a whirl, and, after some thought, I realized there is only one thing that stands the test of time. It is this idea of *companionship*. I mean, a guy and girl can only hold hands and kiss so much. Even if you're a super-lover of mega-kissing (probably not a real thing), you're still going to wind up spending a lot of time with a guy in a platonic, casual way. This means that friendship is going to be really crucial. You must be able to talk and communicate well together. You're going to have to like someone as much as you love him. That's my opinion, but I feel pretty confident about it.

Sure, everyone is looking for romance, love, and affection. But those romantic items alone won't cut it. Those things are far more special if they spill out of a foundation built on friendship. People are built with a burning desire for intimacy, and the root of it is finding a companion to experience life with. This is the connection guys are looking for in everything they do. Friendship is provided to us as the starting point toward intimacy. Without friendship, it's impossible to experience real intimacy.

◇ How does your friendship filter look?
◇ Is friendship at the root of your relationships?
◇ Do your relationships feel more romantic than friendly?
◇ Are you feeling more pressure or more encouragement in your relationships?
◇ Are you and your boyfriend compatible as great friends?

◇ Do you two actually have things in common that take up lots of time together?

GUY TIP

The truth is that what a guy most wants in a girl is someone who cares, knows, loves, supports, and laughs with him. In other words, a true friend. I realize some people and some magazines might not agree or might try to minimize statements like this. But the basis for any good relationship is the ability to be a good friend. We just need to realize what it takes to be one.

Real friends have the ability to challenge, change, and inspire you. Are you willing to let those things happen? Friends care enough to be honest with you even when they know your faults. Friends will call to see how you're doing—not just to see what's going on. Friends know when you're hurting and will be there to listen—without expecting anything in return. Real friends don't look to get stuff out of the relationship for themselves. They're willing to put your needs above their own—but also appreciate that real friendship goes both ways.

JESUS' SIBLINGS AND WHATNOT

I recently read something in a book I really appreciated. And I didn't even like the rest of the book, but this part I liked greatly:

True friends don't spend time gazing into each other's eyes. They may show great tenderness towards each other, but they face in the same direction—toward common projects, goals—above all, towards a common Lord.

—C. S. Lewis

The book talked about how much better off teens might be if they stopped treating each other like potential dates. What if guys and girls tried to see and treat each other like brothers and sisters in Christ? I thought about it for a while, and then a while longer. What if we really did stop thinking so much in terms of romance and love and just started viewing others as if they were brothers or sisters? Well . . . without the violent brother-sister dynamic that happened to me.

I think that if guys and girls would try this, they could see one another in a different light. Instead of seeing other people for what they can offer, they could view people as valuable people simply because they *are* valuable. They would stop seeing them for what they might be able to do for them—which is a selfish way to think about people, by the way. Not only would we appreciate others to a greater extent, but the people being valued would feel more important too.

Give it some thought. If you didn't look at the opposite sex through the lens of romance and love first, but instead started looking at guys through the lens of friendship and care, perhaps all of your relationships would become stronger. I can't predict your future, but I'd be willing to bet that this lens is a good one and will help you see relationships and people more accurately. And good vision is important, especially when it concerns people.

---------------▷ DISCUSSION STUFF ◁---------------

1. Name the first three guys who come to your mind. What do you think they most want from girls? Is it good or bad? Does this say anything about you?

2. Are there some long-term characteristics of guys that would be good to think about that you have not thought about before? Why haven't you included them before?

3. What are the long-term characteristics you think guys are looking for in girls? Why do you think they are drawn to these traits?

4. Have you ever idolized a guy—that is, put him up on a pedestal and overlooked some obvious character flaws?

5. What traits are you attracted to in guys that could backfire or be harmful to you in the short term and the long term?

6. What filters do you use to weed out guys who are unhealthy to be around versus guys who are healthy to be around?

7. Are there ways you need to value the guys and girls around you more?

chapter 13

GUYS HAVE SECRETS

Everyone has secrets; that's not a secret. But maybe the details are. A lot of the time these things that we keep secret isolate us. We think maybe we are the only ones. But the truth is there are all kinds of questions, quirks, habits, struggles, addictions, or just questions that make people feel isolated. Perhaps pulling back the curtain on a few of the things that guys deal with will be helpful.

Our Secret and Not-So-Secret Struggles

Guys and girls often have unique struggles because of their genders. Sure, there are plenty of issues that are the same. And there are some struggles that are more common for girls, like self-image, insecurity, jealousy, and gossip. And of course, all issues cross the gender lines from time to time.

For guys the three most common struggles are controlling sexual desire, greed, and anger. They are always there, knocking at our door. They're the top three plays of the week.

⇨ LUST

I actually don't like this word. Some people feel awful or ashamed of their sexual desires. I don't think we should. They are totally natural and biological. But learning to control them and to not be controlled *by* them is a different matter. This is a tough one for most guys because of all the ridiculous ways that boobs and butts are constantly marketed to them. Between the commercials, magazine, and catalog advertisements, billboards, the Internet, and girls' clothes—it can overstimulate the physical senses. It can easily become overwhelming and obsessive. And the same things that make guys appreciate a girl's wonder and beauty can morph into a harmful, addictive way to think about women.

⇨ GREED

Money is power. I always think it's strange when I hear about another guy who has 50 million dollars stealing another 100 million dollars in some Wall Street scam. It's not the money that is controlling him. It is the power and influence that money represents. Guys sense that at a very early age. It starts in the form of simple competition. As we grow, we see how that translates into the stuff we're good at, and it can become a very bad habit. For a guy, the power to compete lasts a lifetime. It's not a bad thing, but most bad things are good things in the wrong amounts or at the wrong times. After high school and college, guys continue to compete with one another by trying to obtain more power, control, and money. Since money is a powerful way to control things, it can become like a drug. A powerful, stupid drug.

⇨ ANGER

Ever see a bull sitting in a rodeo chute? Sometimes guys are full of testosterone and energy with no place to direct it. They become a bit like that bull in the rodeo chute. Sometimes when guys can't figure something out or become over-whelmed, it can cause anger, rage, fighting, and all that odd, aggressive stuff you see guys doing on occasion. Whatever the reasons may be, anger can be an ongoing problem that lots of guys struggle with.

SIMPLE OR COMPLEX?

Do you think the guys you know are fairly simple beings or more complex? Here's what one counselor had to say: "Guys often joke about females being hard to understand, but it's rare for girls to laugh about the mysterious ways of guys. Maybe that's because girls don't realize that guys are complex. When a girl only takes a guy at face value, she may unknowingly sabotage a potential friendship with him before it has time to develop. Or, she may end up feeling hurt unnecessarily."[1]

That's what happens in the following story.

I had a huge crush on Andy. He was all I thought about. He seemed interested in me too. When he said he'd call, I stayed home that night and expected him to call. I wasn't going to miss it for anything! But the hours dragged by, and the phone didn't ring. Finally, when I couldn't stand waiting any longer, I called him. He was nice but seemed eager to get off the phone. I could hear his friends laughing in the background. Andy was having fun without me. I was annoyed and hurt.

Here she is, feeling left out and hurt, while Andy doesn't seem to be suffering much without her at all.

How do you know if a guy is interested or not? Here are a few insights about guys that might help answer that question, as well as a few other questions you might have . . .

Guys' Lives Don't Revolve Around Girls

I hate to break any hearts here, but this is kind of important. Guys don't think about girls all day. Don't get me wrong. Guys think about girls. A lot, in fact. But even if they are interested in a girl, most guys still want to have plenty of fun with other people too. Teenage guys don't depend on relationships the same way girls do. They tend to have more of a balance in the things they do, like sports and hobbies, their accomplishments and jobs, and in spending time with their other guy friends. During teen years, guys place a high value on the camaraderie of other guys. Which brings up another secret . . .

Guys Like Breathing Room

Guys don't appreciate it when girls isolate them from their friends. There's almost nothing that gets to a guy more than a girl who takes him away from his friends or makes him feel bad about wanting to be with his friends. A girl with a special interest in a guy would be wise not to insist on occupying all, or even too much, of his time.

There's an added benefit to being nonpossessive around guys. It makes you more desirable in return, as strange as it might seem. When a girl is relaxed and enjoying life with others, it makes her that much more attractive.

Guys Are Vulnerable

It was a myth that the earth is flat. It is also a myth that guys are hard-hearted. People may casually call them simple, cold, tough, and unemotional, but that's not true.

It's true that most guys don't think about their dream girls and love all day long. Gross. But they are capable of deeply caring for a girl and getting hurt just as easily as you can. In some cases these emotions can be even more painful for guys to experience because society doesn't provide them the same freedom to vent their feelings. As a result, they don't express themselves easily and keep a lot inside. But their emotions are still there!

The way a guy responds to his feelings is different from the way a girl handles them. Guys go to great lengths to avoid being mocked or ridiculed. Instead of crying or confiding in a buddy, a guy is more likely to do something physical, like shooting hoops or hitting a punching bag.

SHHH!

Most teen guys instinctively behave in a way that shows they aren't ready for marriage. Because, well, they are not. And their sometimes confusing behavior (to a girl) is there to display through their actions that they aren't ready for deep relationships. So they hang out with their buddies more as a coping mechanism. Simply put, more time with a girl equals a more serious relationship. The more serious it gets, the more likely it's going to lead to the idea of marriage or a severely broken heart. So avoiding these types of talks or relationships is sort of like a guy's way of subconsciously protecting himself. And by doing that, a guy winds up protecting you as well as himself.

Here's some advice straight from teen guys. It isn't the deepest advice in the world, but it may help you learn a little more about them.

◈ Don't always ask guys what they're thinking unless you're prepared to discuss topics such as navel lint, fire, football formations, and awesomely stupid jokes.

◈ If you ask a question you don't really want an answer to, expect the answer you don't want to hear.

◈ Sometimes guys are not thinking about you. Live with it.

◈ If guys are going somewhere, absolutely anything they wear is fine. Really.

♦ Crying feels like blackmail to guys.

♦ Ask for what you want. Let's be clear: Subtle hints don't work. Strong hints don't work. Really obvious hints don't work. Just say it!

♦ Guys are not mind-readers, and they never will be. Their lack of mind-reading ability is not an indication that they don't care or think about you.

♦ "Yes" and "no" are perfectly acceptable answers to almost every question.

♦ It's neither in your best interest nor in theirs to take any quiz together.

♦ You can either ask guys to do something or tell them how you want it done. Not both.

♦ If guys ask what's wrong and you say "nothing," they will act like nothing's wrong. They know you're lying, but it's just not worth the hassle. Say what you mean.

♦ If guys say something that can be interpreted in two ways and one of those ways makes you angry, they meant the other way.

▷ DISCUSSION STUFF ◁

1. In what ways is your biology conflicting with your ideology?

2. What are some things that you think guys secretly struggle with? Does this change your view of them, and if so, how?

3. Why do you think guys get so angry sometimes? In what ways is anger natural, and in what ways do you think it becomes unhealthy?

4. Are there ways that you have oversimplified guys? If so . . . how?

5. What myths about guys might you be questioning? Why?

6. What are some things that guys in your life might be struggling with that you might be able to think about and identify now although you couldn't before?

chapter 14

DATING ADVICE FROM GUYS

The purpose of opening a door for a girl is not that she can't do it for herself. It's not about a guy asserting his power and authority. It's about a guy showing honor and respect for you. When he asks you out, pays for stuff, and opens doors for you, it's just his way of showing you that you're valued. It's not about him. It's about his being selfless and thinking about you. Sometimes these small gestures can tell you something much bigger about his character.

WHO ASKS WHO OUT?

Do you believe in equal rights? I kind of hope you don't. Well, not entirely at least. I don't think we really want to have guys and girls doing all of the exact same things. When two people dance, one of them has to lead; otherwise, they'll both wind up with bruised feet and looking sort of stupid. Neither will enjoy the dance.

Sometimes guys and girls have different roles. Otherwise, why have different genders? Why wouldn't God just make us one being who can get itself pregnant and be kind of asexual that way? There is a reason why there are males and females. They do different things, and then when you put them together, they make a good team. If they try. As it turns out, most girls prefer that guys ask them out. So don't lower your standards just because you feel the desire or pressure to be the one running after the boy. Girls who do this are usually afraid that the thing they want will pass them by if they don't get it any way they can. But the ends do not always justify the means. Don't think that guys have given up on romance. Following the crowd is usually just a matter of the blind following the blind.

Don't get me wrong. I'm not saying that girls should never ask a guy out under any circumstance. Occasionally, I have seen it work out. But it's safe to say that it just tends to work out a lot better, flow a little easier, and be more romantic if the guy does the asking. Here's why: guys need to work up the courage to do it. They aren't born with confidence; they need to develop it.

SHHH!

As much as guys want to act confidently, it takes a lot of nerve to ask a girl out. So let guys do this part. Think of courage and confidence as muscles. It's not a good idea to keep guys from building the muscles they will need their entire lives. It also lets you know that they are interested in you, and that they're willing to stick their necks out to hear your answer of yes or no.

Deciding yes or no is one of those privileges that girls get. If I were a girl I would probably not throw that one away.

There are plenty of girls who don't see why who asks who out is a big deal. Sometimes I hear them say that what's important is learning about each other after. And while there is some truth in that, there is also truth in the way guys view girls who ask them out. If a guy can see that a girl is already really interested in him, it may change his whole opinion of her.

Another reason to let guys do the asking is that a guy feels good about himself when he finally musters up the courage to ask a girl out and she says yes. Because he has risked something and gotten a reward, he will now put more effort into the whole thing.

It's a good rule of thumb to let guys do the instigating. It doesn't mean that you both can't enjoy the dance. It just means that things may go smoother if each person knows his or her part of the dance. Besides, girls are always complaining that guys should learn to dance properly.

THE GROUP THING

I'm convinced that the most important thing you can get out of dating in high school is the appreciation for deep friendship.

With historical certainty, you and your high school sweetheart probably won't marry each other. Sorry, but the data doesn't lie. So why put more of your heart into the relationship than you should? Take some of the dating pressure off and do things in groups.

Getting together in groups is a great way to get to know each other and have fun doing it. You can see how the guy reacts around you and your friends. You can learn almost everything you need to know about people from watching their behavior. Wanna see how a guy treats you? Well then, see how the guy treats you in the presence of others. You'll get to see how he treats your friends. It can be really difficult to fall hard for someone and then discover he doesn't act the same way around other people. Who needs that? Not you, that's who.

It's also a lot safer to date in groups. There really is safety in numbers, and there's also safety in the comfort and company of friends. You're free to relax with your friends while you get to know the guy you're going out with. That way, if the guy is being a tool or things don't go that well, you're still with other people you can have a great time with. When a guy and girl find themselves falling head over heels for each other—that's called *infatuation*, by the way—it can be hard to live up to the purity standards you hopefully have. Also, set high standards beforehand, now that I think about it.

What You Don't Owe Guys

May I remind you of something? Thanks so much. You don't owe anything about your body to anyone. Not your hands, your lips, or any other part of your body. Just because you spend time with someone, and just because he might do things for you or buy food for you, doesn't mean that you owe a guy anything. You aren't obligated to kiss him, touch him, allow him to put his arm around you, or even let him hold your hand.

When you say yes to going out on a date, you should show the guy the respect of your time and attention. That's all you "owe." And really that's just being considerate.

Lots, and I mean lots, of girls feel pressure from guys while on a date. They'll give in to guys because they feel uncomfortable or insecure about saying no. Some guys are big, and they can be pushy and extremely intimidating. Girls can be afraid of making guys mad or worry that guys won't like them in return. To be honest, what that really indicates is that a girl doesn't know her own value and worth. Don't ever be so concerned about pleasing other people that you sacrifice your own worth in the process.

Girls like diamonds and other fancy, pretty stuff, because these things are rare, expensive, and hard to get. Don't be a semiprecious stone. Who wants to be called *semi* anything?

Saying no doesn't make you a prude. It doesn't make you come across as shallow, a religious nut, or too uptight. The more you demand respect, give respect, and set yourself apart from other girls, the more the right guy will want to put forth the time and effort to show you the respect and care you deserve. And if you didn't let that last sentence soak in, try reading it again.

→ GUY TIP ←

If a guy sees that physical things come easily with you, he'll wind up disappointed in the long run. Think about it. Anticipation is what makes Christmas morning so exciting. It's the anticipation that keeps guys interested in a girl sometimes. In the meantime, you can both get to know the person in front of you. The real person with the heart and dreams and feelings. You want a guy to end up deeply caring for you, not just wanting to see what you look like under your clothes. It's the cheap thrill versus the heart thrill.

Be a diamond in the rough. Don't put yourself on display at the discount store for any guy with a little bit of time and some money.

HONOR AND REGRET

Most girls don't fully understand what's going on when it comes to sex. Well, guys don't really get it either. When a girl is considering sex, she often justifies it by saying "but I love him," even if she doesn't want to go through with it. Why?

The girl pictures marrying the guy someday. The guy pictures everything he wants to do with the girl before he goes back to tell his buddies all about it. Most likely he has no dreams of groomsmen or his honeymoon in this scenario. Go ahead, ask around if you don't believe me. Now I'm going to tell you something very, very simple that I hope you will believe:

Guys and girls have sex for very, very different reasons. Especially the younger they are. Guys and girls experience sex differently, and they think about it differently.

> Guys + sex = physical pleasure motive
> Girls + sex = love motive

Now, it doesn't mean guys will never equate love and sex, nor does it mean that girls won't ever want sex for physical pleasure. But it absolutely does mean that the first motive for sex will affect the outcome and your understanding of it completely.

Why does a guy act like sex is less than a huge love experience? For two reasons. First, the physical pleasure is no doubt a big plus for him. Second, intimacy comes with maturity, and you cannot be an adult when you are still a kid. Some things have to age before they become what they're meant to be. Cheese, wine, and probably guys.

/////////////// **WARNING!** ///////////////

Guys want to be honorable. Even if they don't think about that a lot now, they will later. Being honorable is part of being strong, and every guy wants to feel strong. Living with no regrets is better than trying to convince yourself that you don't regret the decisions you've made. There's a big difference.

//

Avoid Traps

It's just as important to avoid bad things as it is to look for good things. This is especially relevant in the romance world. While it's great to be hopeful, it's not great to be naive. Also, naive spelled backwards spells Evian. I'm just saying.

Avoid bedrooms: As a teen, your bedroom is for sleeping and throwing your dirty laundry on the floor, not for getting to know your boyfriend. Guys have strong associations to things. If they're in a relaxed setting with a bed, they're going to associate you with that situation. You're better off staying out of the bedroom except for sleeping (alone—and duh). Thought I'd just clarify.

Stay in public: Girls don't usually get pressured or physically abused in public places. So make sure you get to decide where you want to go on dates—and make sure you go someplace where you and the guy will be around other people. Trust me, you're a lot safer that way. This is part of not being naive.

Skip the party scene: Over 90 percent of the time that teenage sexual activity takes place, alcohol or drugs are involved.[1] Dating is about getting to know each other, not about partying and drinking. Alcohol distorts reality. If you like each other, why distort your physical reality? If you and the guy don't like each other much, why are you going out in the first place? Nothing good can come from teenage drinking or drug use, so avoid that stuff altogether. These substances confuse reality; they don't clarify it.

The creepy dude: You may not always know someone well when you're asked out on a date. If that's the case, don't accept a random invitation from him, even if he doesn't seem creepy. If you don't really know someone or, more important, his character, then don't say yes to a date, and certainly don't fly solo. If you do accept an invitation to go out, then agree only if he's willing to double-date or go out with a group of your friends or just have coffee in public or something simple. You can still have a great time. After getting to know him better, then you can decide if he's nice enough to see again, or if the dude just needs to move on without you.

That's Somebody Else's Wife

Most of the girls I had crushes on or dated are now married to other men or will be soon. When I try and put myself into the shoes of those men, it makes me think more about respecting women so that they bring joy and optimism into their marriages. You don't want to be a part of someone else's baggage.

This also works the other way around. I'll think the same thing about my wife in the future. I'll hope that people treated her well so that she is healthy and optimistic about love and guys and life.

What about you? Do you like the idea of someone else being with your future husband? Take it a step further. After you're married and have your own children, how will you feel about a guy taking advantage of your daughter?

I see girls from a very different perspective now. Mostly because I spend a lot of time around them and their giggliness at things like the Revolve Tour. Seriously, every one of you is someone's daughter. You're someone's future wife. You were each made to be a treasure, perhaps someday to be shared in a very special relationship with a very special someone.

MEET MY DAD

Hopefully your dad is involved in your life. And maybe you are lucky enough to have the encouraging, protective, and involved father. If so, be sure to introduce the guy you are dating to your parents, especially to your dad.

> If, by chance, your dad has big arms, tell him to wear a tight T-shirt, just to let the guy know that those arms could hurt his face if he hurts his daughter. Your date would do the same thing for his daughter when the time comes.

I'm not asking you to set up a double date with your folks. The point is this. You are not your own. It's good sometimes to let the guy know that you are someone's very important daughter. When a guy sees the person who loves and protects you, buys your clothes and your food, and is involved in your life, the date will be different. Here's why. He thinks of you as someone's daughter and not just his date. He takes into consideration that it's not about getting what he wants from you, but instead he thinks about you in relation to your family.

Here's a little more advice. You may not want to get a guy too involved with your family too quickly. Sometimes that creates a bond that can make a guy feel locked into the relationship with you too fast. Just make sure that he knows your parents are there for you and involved. Show him that your family is important to you and that you expect him to treat you with the care and respect that not only you, but also your family, demand.

GOD AND SEX

I discovered something that outdoes sex. Something and Someone. It's God.

Here's the good news. I love that the story of God is a love story to people and a story about forgiveness and redeeming hearts and minds. I have regrets about the way I treated girls when I was young. I was a lost and confused kid, like a lot of others. But it is purifying to know that God has forgiven me and changed me, and he is in the process of changing my heart every day, filling it with more love and understanding. Well, most days, unless I'm being an idiot and not listening.

I realize that some of you reading these words have already made mistakes in your relationships. Plenty of people don't like or relate to words like *purity*. Some people have done things that were stupid when they weren't thinking. If you are currently sexually active with your boyfriend, or if you have been sexually active in the past, you can always change your behavior. God is constantly offering you the encouragement to make better decisions and love better. No matter what you've done in the past, with God's help, you can always improve your future.

God is love. And God is the author of sex, love, and relationships. (In fact, sex is only one type of physical love.) God created these things for us to enjoy when we fully follow his design for how things should be done. I've come to discover that God is not a "moralizer." He doesn't say "Do this" or "Don't do that" for no reason. Everything he tries to help us understand or do or avoid is done in love—even when we don't see it or think that there should be restrictions. He's saying it because he loves us, and it's in our best interest. He's saying it because he knows how he built us, knows what's best for us, and knows what will bring us the *most* fulfillment. And you know what? From where I'm sitting . . . that's a pretty great father figure.

──────▷ DISCUSSION STUFF ◁──────

1. Who should ask whom out? Why?
2. Discuss the role that confidence plays in guys approaching girls, both as teens and how it affects them later in life.
3. Are there ways that you might actually enjoy high school more by putting less emphasis on romance? What might that look like?
4. If you realize that you probably won't marry anyone you date in high school, does that affect the way you date?
5. How do the purity standards that you set for yourself play themselves out when it comes to guys?
6. Have you let guys take advantage of you or guilt you into anything before? If so, why do you think you gave in? How would you do things differently now?
7. How might your view of sex be different from that of guys?

Barbie and GI Joe

> {
> Wisdom is the most important
> thing; so get wisdom. If it
> costs everything you have, get
> understanding.
>
> —Proverbs 4:7
> }

chapter 15

WHY THEY AREN'T FRIENDS

{
If two people agree on everything,
one of them is unnecessary.

—Anonymous
}

G I Joe and Barbie dashed off to save a soldier being held captive in a jungle hut. They escaped giant explosions and dodged flying bullets as they rescued their friend. Once they had untied him, they snuck out of the hut and jumped into a boat waiting for them to make their escape. They tore down the river and plunged over a waterfall. They were shoved onto dry land by the rush of the white water, just in time to jump into the small cargo plane waiting to take them to safety. As they stumbled into the plane with only a few flesh wounds, Barbie and Joe grabbed each other's hands and squeezed. They'd made it!

The plane delivered them to Barbie's pink convertible. She dropped off their friend and drove to their pretty pink house, where they washed up for dinner. After a luxurious bath, Barbie met Joe in front of the fireplace, where they hugged and kissed as the sun set. Then Barbie showed Joe some new khaki pants she'd bought for him earlier in the day. He tried them on and they fit wonderfully. They had a candlelit dinner and walked in the moonlight. What a day!

OPPOSITES ATTRACT?

Have you seen that episode of GI Joe and Barbie? If you have, please shoot me an e-mail and let me know where I can find it. Actually that might make a good sarcastic cartoon. I'll look into it. But I think if Barbie and GI Joe ever hung out, one of them would end up dead. I don't mean just *slightly* dead. I mean dead like super dead. Why? Because they are complete opposites. And probably one of them would just end up throwing the other off a cliff and calling it an accident.

Think about it. Barbie—who is what? . . . proportionally nine feet tall in her pink sequin airline attendant outfit—wouldn't exactly fit in with jungle machetes, grenades, mud, and really bad body odor. Not to mention good old Joey, who would have a pretty hard time at Barbie's tea parties while hanging out in the Hamptons. I highly doubt he'd be willing to wear pink polo shirts with checkered shorts underneath all of his camouflage.

Can you just picture it? GI Joe, Barbie, and her other man, Ken, sitting around, drinking iced tea at patio parties, then jogging in slow motion along the beach together? Maybe Ken could show Joe how to pop his collar and tie a sweater around his waist or shoulders. Joe could show Ken how to go to the bathroom in the jungle, where the best spots are to bury their waste, how to eat bark, and the best techniques for crawling around in the mud. Maybe they could top it all off by rigging a raccoon with some explosives and blowing up a shack of terrorists or something.

To be honest, I don't know why someone hasn't brought these three characters together already. It's a match made in heaven.

Sooo . . . what I'm really saying is I don't have to tell you why Barbie and GI Joe aren't friends. They're just too entirely different. They don't exist in the same world. And while they don't really resemble everything that goes on between guys and girls, they do serve to illustrate one very important point. Guys and girls are very different.

This is a fact that we often underestimate. Sure, there are similarities. We all like to eat, we all sleep, we all want to be loved, and we may even have a fondness for kittens or puppies. Most of us laugh a little when someone falls down. I'm not saying that's okay. Hmm . . .

Guys and girls are just different—very different. How are we different? And what's the point of knowing those differences? For starters, it's fun and makes more sense of our lives! You don't have cooties anymore, and you're probably fascinated by the opposite sex. Don't worry. You're not alone, and it's normal.

IT'S A MYSTERY!

The truth is, your sexuality—as a guy or girl—affects your behavior. The way you display these differences makes you distinctly male or female. I'm not telling you what to do with these differences. I'm just saying they are there. There is a purpose for even the smallest differences between guys and girls. But we'll get to that later.

YOU JANE . . . ME TARZAN

Here are some simple yet odd things that I've noticed about the differences between most girls and guys:

1. Girls generally use restrooms as social experiences. Guys won't speak a word or even make eye contact with other guys they don't know while using them. However, girls can meet, cry, share life experiences, and laugh together like old friends by the time they leave.
2. A girl's hair can be fourteen inches long, yet she expects her friends to notice when it is cut by just a quarter of an inch.
3. When a girl looks in the mirror, she will often focus on one tiny imperfection. She may obsess about one area of her body that she thinks is too fat. A dude, on the other hand, can be three hundred pounds, white as a ghost, with odd body hair, and smell like something awful, but will focus on the one developed area of his biceps.

4. A guy will pay two bucks for an item only worth one if he really needs it. A girl will pay one dollar for a two-dollar item that she doesn't need, because it looks so cute and it's on sale.

5. A guy may have up to five items in his bathroom. The average number of items in a girl's bathroom is reported to be as high as 437.

6. A guy's handwriting is often ugly and unreadable. Do you know what else? We're okay with it. In fact, I can safely say that most of us even like it. Girls, on the other hand, will pull out their scented markers and matching stationery and use these enormous loops to finish off every letter. And just so you know, it's hard to understand what a girl is saying, because even if she's dumping you, she'll finish off her note with a big smiley face and colored hearts at the end.

7. Girls are fascinated by shoes. I offer no explanations. It confuses me.

8. Guys have lots of gas. Girls don't usually enjoy it. I have a couple of friends who do, but it kinda weirds me out, to be honest. What they don't know, however, is that for every bit of gas that slips out, the guy has probably held it in for fifteen minutes, enduring a decent amount of pain in the process. Seriously, it's uncomfortable.

These are just a few differences to kick around and start thinking about when it comes to guys and girls. Let's proceed with a few more, a bit more in-depth.

Room to Groom

Without looking at anybody else, take a look at your finger-nails. Go ahead. Look at them. Okay, how did you do it? Did you extend your hand out flat with your palm facing down to look at your nails? Did you look at both hands? The fact is, about eight in ten times, girls will look at their hands this way.

All I really asked you to do is look at your nails, but what did you do? You probably looked at the entire presentation—your hands, your fingers in proportion to your hands, your fingers in comparison to your nails, the jewelry adorning your wrists and fingers, the cuticles surrounding your nails, whether or not you have a hangnail, and possibly the color of your nails and how the polish looks. You may have even looked at all of this in proportion to your arms, along with the tone and shade of your skin on your arms—how long your arms are, if you need more sun, and how your shirt balanced everything else out—because, after all, it is the closest thing you're wearing that may have an effect on your nails, particularly if they are polished.

> People throw away what they could have by insisting on perfection, which they cannot have, and looking for it where they will never find it.
>
> —Edith Schaeffer

You get my point, hopefully. Ask a guy to look at his finger-nails. What will he do? About eight in ten will curl their fingers into their palms, then turn their palms upward and bring their nails close to their face. They will look at their fingernails only because you asked them to do it. What they will not do is have a clue as to why they are supposed to be looking at them. Guys don't color-coordinate, and most of them don't even know what cuticles are. They look at their nails and say, "Yep, they're nails. Neato. Nails. Now what?" Now, don't worry if you happened to do it that way too. It's not like you're a freak or anything. The point is that, in general, girls tend to be into grooming a whole lot more than guys. It doesn't take a ton of research to figure that out. Just smell a guy after he hasn't showered for a day. Or don't.

If you have a brother, the odds are that your room smells way better than his room does. You have more nail polish and hairbrushes, that's for certain. Guys don't care about their physical appearance to the same degree, on average.

THE TREAT AND GREET

These differences between guys and girls come out even with their greetings. There's the crazy, high-pitched, screaming "Hello!" that girls do. And then there's the guys' back-slapping, high-five, one-arm-hug, ghetto gangsta greeting.

For example, I was in a coffee shop when two girlfriends saw each other. I'm guessing they hadn't seen each other in quite a while. Immediately, their voices went from calm to a freakish, high-pitched, alien-intriguing, dogs'-ears-hurt squeal. At least that's what it sounded like to me. They would probably call it excitement and happiness. They jumped up and down and squealed some more. Allegedly they weren't fighting, but I couldn't tell if someone wasn't maybe being assaulted. They were just saying hi.

Girls and guys greet each other in incredibly different ways. Guys usually say hi with smaller amounts of emotional reaction and guarded body language. We do this especially as teenagers. We don't have the same confidence in expressing our emotions that girls have. Intro the casual head nod.

Don't forget the turn-it-into-a-fist, finger-trickle-off way guys shake hands. If guys hug, it's not really an embrace. It's this weird, awkward, try-to-be-cool-looking slapping of the hands between us, while we grab the guy's shoulder with the other hand. What's important is not so much to embrace, but to pat each other two or three times on the back—and violently. It's as if the embrace says, "I love you, but I might hit you too."

PYROS

Why in the world are guys so obsessed with fire . . . and then there's blowing stuff up . . . shooting off fireworks . . . or just shooting in general—paintball, BB guns, arcade games, and laser tag? Why don't most girls try to set things on fire, make contraptions that blow things up, or try to put M-80s into blue-gills to see how far their guts will fly?

There's a reason. Most guys are more drawn to riskier activities. We like taking risks. We like the adrenaline spike. When we're excited, but scared at the same time, we feel very alive and engaged. Being in thrilling and dangerous situations is a way a guy builds confidence, overcomes fears, and feels stronger. Sure, it's a little strange to a lot of girls, but it's an important way for a guy to find his identity as he becomes a man.

I don't mean to break any hearts here, and I doubt I will,

but a guy is not someone who is just kind, sweet, and smells good all the time. He also longs to be passionate, strong, enduring. A warrior of sorts. You know that guy in movies who gives speeches before leading his men into certain death? There's a reason that is appealing to guys.

Guys do all kinds of stuff that might seem weird or odd to you, but know that it does have a place. After all, you do all kinds of stuff that we think is pretty strange too. But if guys are GI Joe and girls are Barbie, then we have to learn to get along despite the differences. He must wash his dirty hands and eat with a fork, and she might wear a camouflage dress to dinner. Hey, will that doll sell?

So What Do I Do with That?

There are lots of differences between girls and guys, and we could go on about them forever. Some are fun, some are goofy, and some have seemingly nothing to do with answers to most girls' questions about guys. But there is a bigger point.

If guys and girls look at fingernails differently, imagine how differently we see everything else. We probably see dating differently. We probably carry our emotions differently. We most likely have different ways of loving one another and being loved by one another. The bottom line is that guys and girls will act, think, and feel differently than their counterparts.

A lot of people look at differences negatively. Sure, some of them you can laugh about. But most everyone draws his or her own conclusion about things that are different before trying to understand them.

You may not understand why a guy won't open up to you about what he's thinking. Maybe you're confused about why he gives you little gifts when all you really want are his words. For that guy, those gifts are the words you're seeking. That's because guys and girls communicate in different languages. That code just needs to be unlocked and understood for each person. It is hard sometimes, but it's worth it too.

The more we understand one another, the better off we'll be. Maybe more important, this stuff relates to advice we get from the Bible. Take a look at the different ways Jesus was able to communicate with and relate to people. He didn't do it through differences. He always got to the heart of the matter.

In one story, Jesus' disciples were trying to preach to some townspeople. It wasn't going well. People weren't listening. They were getting violent, angry, and hostile. What did Jesus do in response? Jesus looked at them and had compassion. People were throwing things at him and trying to violently hurt him, and his response was compassion. Jesus saw them as "sheep without a shepherd" (Matthew 9:36). They were lost and didn't understand, and his response was to care.

Jesus didn't walk away from people because of differences. And if he didn't walk away while being punched and kicked, I'm sure we can all do better.

GUY TIP

The next time a guy is acting weird, annoying, or just plain different . . . stop and look at him the way Jesus looked at people. Try to understand *why* he is behaving that way, not just that he *is* behaving that way.

Mirror, Mirror on the Wall . . .

You've gotten a lot of information so far. Before you head into the remaining chapters, stop to catch your breath. Take a few minutes to reflect on the answers to these questions:

- ♦ When you look in the mirror, who do you see?
- ♦ Do you ever have trouble seeing people as Jesus sees them? Why?
- ♦ What do you want guys to see when they look at you? How does your faith affect that?
- ♦ What are the three most important things you are looking for in a relationship?
- ♦ What are the three things that scare you the most about relationships?
- ♦ What's your idea of an ideal relationship?

────────▷ Discussion Stuff ◁────────

1. What are some issues that guys and girls always have a difficult time agreeing about?
2. What are some things guys do that drive you crazy? More important, why do they bother you?
3. What is another difference between guys and girls that isn't covered in this chapter?
4. What is a difference about guys that you actually appreciate, that you might not have thought of before? Why do you appreciate this difference?
5. If Jesus still loved people who threw rocks at him, spit on him,

and kicked him, how can you be more accepting of some of the differences that people have in your life? (Warning: this does not mean that it is ever okay for a guy or anyone else to hurt you.)

6. How does the way you view yourself affect your expectations of guys, or other girls, in your life?

chapter

THE THING ABOUT EYEBALLS

{
Our eyes work . . . usually more
than we ask them to.

—Chad
}

Like so many other girls, Rachel has a problem. Guys confuse her.

What is wrong with guys!? Ahhh!! It's like the only thing they want is to get something from you or hook up. They don't care about anything else! I'm not a slut, and I don't have a sign around my neck advertising sex. I just want a guy who likes me for who I am, and someone I can care about. Why do I always attract such jerks?

—Rachel

145

It's Easier Than You Think

While Rachel's assertions about guys aren't exactly factual, her feelings are valid. A lot of girls feel this way and are equally confused about why they seem to be magnets for guys with jerk behavior. Every wonder why? Why do some girls attract no guys? Some get the slightly strange ones. Other girls try really hard and attract guys who usually aren't the most upstanding of character. And other girls seem to effortlessly attract pretty good guys. I'll bet if I were a girl, this would be pretty frustrating to me too. But luckily for all of us, there are reasons why these things happen. And you can understand some of them pretty easily. And knowledge is pretty powerful if you put it to use. How's that for a pep speech?

Here's my point. Many times (emphasis on *many*) guys hear girls talking about their frustrations with guys. Girls are hurt or annoyed that guys obsess about the physical attributes and don't focus on the heart or personality of a girl. It's as though girls feel like they are magnets for creepy, immature, self-centered guys.

So turn off that "girl brain" for a minute and try to look at things through a guy's eyes. It really helps sometimes.

Hey There, Creepy Memory . . .

Mike is twelve, going on thirteen, and hanging out with some buddies. One of the guys pulls out a *Playboy*. Mike's heart starts beating very quickly at the sight of those images, a reaction he doesn't even intentionally try to have. For the first time, he sees a naked, smiling, flawless (airbrushed), inviting, seemingly perfect woman. She is just lying there, inviting him in with her smile. This is a significant moment. Mike's brain is forever different.

Now Mike is sixty-five. Yes, sixty-five. More than fifty-two years have passed since that memorable day. There is something about Mike's brain that might shock you. Mike's brain can still recall about thirteen different parts of that picture he saw when he was just a teenager. And do you want to know what he remembers most? Her personality and smile.

Seriously? No. Did you really consider that for real? If you did . . . that's cute. Also naive. He remembers the physical aspects of her body. And there is a reason why.

It can be very hard to understand how a guy's brains can have such a lasting memory of an experience so small, so long ago. Maybe it doesn't concern you a great deal, or maybe it fascinates or grosses you out to know that.

So why are guys so seemingly obsessed with girls' bodies? Is that all they care about? Well, in some ways no, and in others, YES! The yes happens especially if girls bring disproportionate attention to the physical aspects of them. And you know what I mean. If a girl is always advertising the booty and whatever else attracts male attention, then yes, guys will mostly be drawn to that aspect. And it's not about whether or not it should be one-piece bathing suits or bikinis; it's an unspoken attitude of physical availability that guys are usually confused by. And sometimes a guy's eyes and heart can be put in conflict with each other.

All of guys' decisions aren't completely up to them. Some actually are influenced by you, especially the ones that concern your body. I'll try explaining another way.

Imagine that you are a guy. A girl walks into an empty

classroom wearing nothing but underwear or a bikini. She walks over and sits down across from you. She wants to talk about her likes and dislikes, favorite movies, books, music, and the kind of dog she owns. She's a really nice girl with a great personality. So what are you thinking about?

SUPER OBVIOUS MOMENT

Answer: Her body! Sex, her curves, legs, lips, skin! Her body says to the guy's brain, "Here I am!" And it can be quite overwhelming. It's partially because of the way guys' brains are wired. All people have two sides to their brains—right and left hemispheres. One is for logical use, and one is for visual, creative, and emotional use. This part is important: If these two things are ever in conflict with each other, in a guy's brain, visual stimuli wins by default 99 percent of the time, and especially for guys in their teens. That means if the girl standing in the room loves puppies and wants to talk about her college application, a guy will probably be too overwhelmed by her body to be able to focus on the other things. None of this means you should be ashamed that a girl's body is attractive to guys. You just have to understand the power a girl's body has over guys so that you don't present it in ways that are unhealthy and lopsided.

GUY TIP

All of this isn't just a matter of willpower. Girls don't know this about guys, but they need you to help them.

Do both the guy and yourself a favor . . . make guys look at you and see something bigger than yourself. Make guys look at you and see God in you.

BUYING WHAT YOU ADVERTISE

Girls like to wear cute outfits. And here is what I know. "Cute" has many, many interpretations. It could mean a sundress and nice shoes. To other people, cute means tiny skirts that show their underwear, or the belly shirt with the visible bra through the mesh, see-through-shirt-whatever-thingy. And I love the "I'm hot for jerks!" T-shirt. Right. And I'm sure that when high school girls post their underwear bathroom pics on their online profiles, the guys who see them are looking straight at their hearts. You wouldn't believe the number of e-mails I get about girls being shocked and hurt after sending nude pictures to their boyfriend, only to find out that he put them online or showed everyone. You simply can't afford to be naive anymore. I mean that.

> When women go wrong, men go right after them.
> —Mae West

Here's where one problem comes into play. And this is pretty significant. Guys are interested in buying what *they* think you are advertising . . . not what *you* think you're advertising. There's a huge difference. Girls may never understand how powerful visual stimuli can be to guys. However, you need to know that *guys are guys*, so if you show and emphasize your body, they'll want your body. It's really that simple. It's extremely hard for them to just talk, hold your hand, listen, and be a gentleman if the message they think you're sending with your body language is "You might be able to get my clothes off."

Most of the girls who are doing this aren't saying this with words, but they are saying it with their bodies, and it's not usually what you even mean! This is where our communication lines cross from what we're saying to what we're doing.

//////////////// **WARNING!** ////////////////

If your body isn't available, don't make it look like it is the item on display. And I'm not talking about bathing suits in the summer. It's more about the tiny-and-scant, sexy-is-the-selling-point, advertising-your-legs-and-stomach look that most girls think of as cute. You may or may not know what you are doing, but you can't be naive anymore.

Guys are already overwhelmed by the mixed messages they get from magazines, shows, and everything else. Their brains don't know how to handle the thousands of confusing messages. They don't need to get a message from a girl that's saying "My body is right here, looking surprisingly out front and available. Aren't I flirty and confident? But more than anything else, please respect me and my heart."

When guys get the message "I'm telling you with my body that I'm available, but I'm telling you with my words that I'm not!", it is very confusing. Plus, guys will always lean toward the message they hear from your body. It's not old-fashioned to respect yourself and your body. And when did modesty become a bad thing? Modesty to many guys actually shows confidence and mystery. And it goes a long way. It doesn't mean that you're "afraid to express yourself." It's feeling confident about who you are and not needing others to affirm your importance.

///

GUY REPELLENT

Here is a fundamental mix-up I often see. If a lot of guys like a girl, then she feels valuable and/or pretty and desired. If a lot of guys—or the guy she is fixated on—don't like her, then she feels less valuable or desirable.

This is what happens when we depend on others to make us feel valuable. It's a tempting trap, but still a trap. Why would you trust someone else's opinion over your own?

It's as though you are giving up on your own opinion of yourself to be judged by others.

Don't get me wrong—it's perfectly natural for all of us to want to be liked by others. When someone finds you attractive, wants to look at you, talk to you, and pay attention to you, it's nice! It's flattering. It's fun! It might help your confidence at times. But in the end, it's usually a sad story. And here is why.

> Women who set a low value on themselves make life hard for all women.
> —Nellie L. McClung

Too many girls want guys to like them. Note that I said *guys*, plural. Not a couple of guys and not *the right* guy, just guys, as though numbers are significant. If this describes you, you might wanna pump those brakes—there's trouble ahead.

Here's a different thought. Maybe a lot of guys don't like you, and that's a great thing. *What? Silly boy, you give dumb advice!* Well, I argue, no, it's good advice. So how can you be likable, attractive, smart, and not have a boyfriend? Maybe this means something else. Instead of attracting lots of people, you are actually repelling the guys who are bad for you.

A lot of girls think they need the attention of lots of guys. This kind of thinking usually has negative effects on your life, your self-worth, and your relationships. Sometimes you need guy repellent.

I mean, think about it. You don't actually *need* tons of guys to be attracted to you. It's not really a healthy or accurate way to interact or think about relationships.

How many guys do you want to marry? How many do you want to date? Ten? Fifty? One hundred and fifty? You don't need tons of guys to like you. You might want a lot of attention sometimes, but you don't *need* it. You need to find your own worth, and it doesn't come from guys. Usually this desperation for affirmation is a telltale sign that you are not comfortable in your own skin.

If you have a healthy self-image, good self-esteem, and find your self-worth in God, you aren't going to look to guys as much to give you value. Besides, they can't create value. They do better at affirming value that already exists. Trust me on that one.

NEWS FLASH!

If you want to find answers, I highly recommend looking at the fatherly aspects of God. They are actually pretty loving and beautiful, to be honest.

You have a natural guy repellent. It comes out by telling guys who you are, and by doing this, you'll naturally attract the people who will be good for you. You'll also repel the people who don't need to be a part of your life.

At the end of the day, you don't need twenty guys feeding you grapes, calling you gorgeous, and playing you love songs. That's kind of weird anyway. You just want one guy—the right guy. One great guy is better than twenty guys who aren't right for you. In fact, anytime twenty guys get together to try to do anything, they usually end up looking kind of awkward. You don't want to be part of that. Trust me.

$\triangleright$ Discussion Stuff $\triangleleft$

---

1. Why do you think that guys are hardwired more toward appearances than girls?
2. If guys want to buy what they think you are advertising, what do you think that they think you are advertising?
3. What percentage of your feeling attractive is based on your physical attributes? Is this healthy or unhealthy?

4. Are you doing things to repel the wrong guys and to attract the right guys?

5. What is one healthy behavior you can implement that will naturally form a more positive attraction in your life?

chapter 17

THAT SEX STUFF

Hey, my name is Eric. You came to my class today to teach us about sex and all that stuff. I really learned a lot. I never realized that so many people get sexually transmitted diseases and all that horrible junk. I don't ever want to get that stuff. I didn't know that there were so many and how easily you could get them. It really makes you think about the girls out there. You just never know if you're really safe. It made me rethink the whole sex thing, and I came to a different decision.

I realize now that if I want to be safe, I just have to nail virgins.

AWWWKWARD!

Yes, if you are wondering, that's a real letter. And if you were a little shocked, then I am glad. I received that letter after he had sat through three days of education about sex, love, and behavior. When I read that letter, I sat back in my chair and just said, "Really?" in a high-pitched kind of voice. Sometimes I'm still surprised at how clueless guys can be about sex. And ya know what? Girls can be too. Welcome to the realities of sex today.

Sex is weird. The act itself takes a lot less time compared to the amount of time people spend thinking about it. It's very disproportionate if you think about it.

But sex is a natural part of life, so it's vital that we try to understand it. You can't avoid it, and you definitely can't ignore it, because it's everywhere.

It's one mean trick to take something natural and beautiful and turn it against us. Like sex. It's good, it's natural, and it's supposed to make life better. But a lot of people don't have that experience. Instead, I usually hear how it is cheapened, it makes your heart hurt, and it doesn't make life better. Sometimes something good and natural, done at the wrong time or in the wrong way, becomes harmful and unnatural. And that's sad. Like when a little puppy gets abandoned on the side of the road sad, but maybe worse. I love puppies.

If I can, I'd like to apologize to you. I am sorry about the way you see sex a lot of the time. I'm sorry for today's culture and the way it paints a picture of love and sex. I'm sorry that there are so many people trying to use sex to sell you a bunch of garbage. I'm sorry that movies and books and the media tell you that sex is anything less than an incredible way to show and feel love.

Because that's what it does. Also it makes babies. Kind of a seriously overlooked outcome.

I'm sorry that you aren't being told how incredibly important and precious you are and how much you have to offer to others just by being you. I'm sorry that adults tell you that you're not in control of your own hormones, and that your sex drive is no more controllable than that of an impulsive monkey, and that there's nothing you can do about it. I'm sorry that people say "Boys will be boys," and that sex is just another part of life, like driving a car or going to the grocery store. The truth is, sex has always been, and will always be, infinitely more important than that. If you will let it be.

Things Treasured

Treat your body, your heart, and your life with as much respect and love as God did when he created you. I mean . . . God is the designer of sex. He knew what he was doing. We're the ones who mess it up.

Sex is so much more than a physical act meeting a physical need. And if I can also say this . . . no matter what you've done or where you've been, God offers a fresh start. You are not a culmination of your mistakes and less-than-great decisions. God is desperately in love with you and is always fighting to win back your love and tell you how loved you already are. God has a plan that includes sex,

> what sex can be, and what it is meant to be. So I guess that brings up the simple question . . .

WHAT IS SEX?

It has been written about in poetry with depth and compassion since time began. It is the reason nations have gone to war. It is an invisible force that often shapes our behavior and curiosity. It's also something cheap and entertaining on TV. It's the punch line of a joke. It's a dirty reference to describe what some guy says he would do to a passing girl. It is something that makes or breaks relationships and marriages. How can we all even be talking about the same thing?

Talking about sex used to be taboo. In the late 1960s and early 1970s, the sexual revolution happened in America. In some ways, it helped society gain a better attitude, or at least the ability to talk about the subject more openly. Before this, sex wasn't something usually brought up as a topic of discussion. It was a hush-hush subject in ways most of us can't imagine. But we went from one end of the spectrum to the other. Although sex has always been an issue, the sexual revolution brought about a newfound openness that led to a decline in personal responsibility and commitment. Since then, sex has seen as less valuable and no longer viewed with the same serious life applications. And this has had consequences. Here are just a few:

- Twenty-five years ago, there were only four sexually transmitted diseases.[1]

- There are now more than fifty common STDs, and the number is growing.[2]
- Half of the infectious diseases in the United States are transmitted sexually.[3]
- One in three of your friends is or will be infected with the human papilloma virus or with genital herpes.[4]
- Seven to 8 percent of teen girls will be pregnant by the age of nineteen, and of those, almost one-third will get an abortion.[5]
- Today's sexually active female teenager is nine times more likely to suffer from depression, anxiety, and suicidal thoughts or attempts.[6]
- One out of four girls is sexually abused at some point in her life.[7]
- More than half of all pregnant teens get pregnant while using some form of contraception.[8]

Sex is everywhere. I've seen it used to sell tires, shampoo, deodorant, and hotels. It's the oldest trick in marketing because it works. Sex is a powerful tool, and it gets used against us every day.

Let's Just Talk and Stuff

Sex is the topic that teens tend to talk about the most and understand the least. Oftentimes a funny thing happens when the subject comes up. I ask guys and girls what they think of first when they think of sex.

Guys usually say something like "Um . . . it's awesome," "It feels good," or "It's what people do to have a baby." Pretty basic answers, really.

Girls usually say things like "Um . . . it's all guys ever think about." Or "It's what people do to have babies." Again, fairly simple answers.

And guys can tell you how to physically have sex in great detail. Which is not awesome to hear about in detail, by the way. They can talk about the female body a lot. But the bottom line is this: they usually think that sex is about the physical act of getting pleasure from the female body.

Sex and Sexuality

A peculiar thing happens as soon as I dip below the surface and ask some deeper questions. The room gets quiet when I ask, "Can you tell me the difference between sex and sexuality? Can you tell me more than two reasons people have sex other than physical pleasure and baby making? Can anyone tell me the difference between love and sexual desire? Can you tell me about the many different types of love there are? What's the purpose of marriage beyond having children and living in the same house? What's the percentage of teens who are have sex and regret it?"

Not only are things quiet, but very few guys have opinions all of a sudden. And those questions aren't even the hard ones.

Sex can be incredibly powerful, or it can be incredibly cheap. It's up to you. One thing that students, especially girls, seem to have a hard time coming to terms with is understanding sexuality. Sexuality is anything that makes you distinctly female or guys distinctly male. Your sexuality is on display all day, every day. You can't help it. It's just part of being human.

//////////////// **WARNING!** ////////////////

Girls aren't always aware of the ways in which they display their sexuality. Most aren't learning about how these ways are different and what to do about it. But you can!

///

First Comes Love . . . Then Comes . . . Marriage?

Let's divert to marriage for a minute. When it comes to marriage, it can be a whole new world of misunderstanding. This is a real tough one. America already has a high divorce rate. The highest divorce rate of any developed nation. This is also true of Christian marriages. When students are asked about the purpose of marriage, not everyone agrees on the answer. And given the ways we have all seen marriage take place, this confusion is totally merited.

A lot of people come from homes where their dad was never around, or their mom and dad had a terrible relationship, or they were abused, or their parents got divorced, or their mom and dad were never available to them.

And this is remarkably sad. The reality, however, is that we are forced to deal with this. If we don't understand the purpose of marriage, why would anyone try to reserve sex only for marriage?

When it comes to understanding sex and why it should

happen only in marriage, we have to think outside the box. Maybe this analogy will help.

Cabin in the Woods: Take One

Imagine that it's a cold winter day. You suddenly find yourself standing in the middle of a forest. You're on your way to a cabin, but it's snowing and getting deep. You've been walking for some time, and now you have to pick up your legs pretty high to step through the deep snow. Your feet are freezing and getting damp. As you breathe in the cold, moist air, it makes your lungs feel like they're burning. Your fingers are getting numb, your ears sting, and you're exhausted!

Finally, in the distance, you see the cabin. You're able to pick up the pace, because you're excited and anxious to get out of the cold. You step up onto the creaky deck and make your way to the door. As you open it up, you instantly feel warmth! You know that inside is a much better place to be. It sure is better than the freezing cold, where your feet and toes feel like they are going to fall off.

As you walk through the door, you immediately notice a large brick wall on the other side of the room. In the center sits a giant fireplace with a big, roaring fire. You shut the door and take a deep breath in and let it out. You smell the cedar wood burning, and it ignites your senses.

You take off your coat, kick the snow off your boots, and lift your freezing feet out of them. It's time to warm your tootsies by the crackling fire. You sit down in a warm, comfortable chair that envelops you as you bask in front of the toasty flames. And

That Sex Stuff

what do you drink if you're warming yourself up in front of the
fire? Hot cocoa, of course! Well, at least that's what my students
almost always say.

What do you have in your delicious hot cocoa? Marshmal-
lows! Why? I think it's because *marshmallow* is a fun word to
say, and we love to squeeze those little suckers and watch them
float around and make our drinks foam.

Now let me ask you a question. In this little scenario in the
cabin, how are you feeling? What are the words that come to
mind to describe your feelings in this situation?

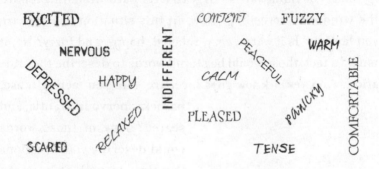

Which words would you choose? Usually, students will
pick words like *relaxed*, *peaceful*, *calm*, *warm*, *happy*, and *fuzzy*
(people love that word). This is a very happy place to be. The
words you think of are positive. In other words, the place that
has been created is a good place to be.

CABIN IN THE WOODS: TAKE TWO

Now, let's do this over. You're back in the woods. Once again,
you're walking through some deep snow on a cold and cloudy

day. Your feet are getting wet and numb. Your legs are tired, and your lungs hurt from breathing in that cold air. Your fingers and ears are freezing, and once again, you're exhausted. You look ahead and see the cabin. You trudge through the snow and make your way there. You step onto the creaky deck and open the door.

Inside, you notice a big, roaring fire waiting for you. Except this time, the fire is in the middle of the room next to the couch, burning through the floor. The flames are rising. Smoke begins to fill the room, and within seconds, the couch is ignited. The flames are so large that they are stretching toward the windows and ceiling! Now, in this situation . . . how are you feeling? Is it warm, cozy, relaxed, happy, and fuzzy? No, it isn't. In fact, those would be stupid words to describe the situation. And yes, I know guys love fire. Are you feeling tense, panicky, nervous, frantic, and scared? Any of those words could describe your emotions this time around. This is not a good situation!

> A successful marriage requires falling in love many times, always with the same person.
> —Mignon McLaughlin

Now here's the big question. Can you see how this scenario relates to sex? Maybe, maybe not, so I'll try to clarify. Teens usually tell me that they have an entirely different set of thoughts and feelings between these cabin examples. But I always say that reaction doesn't make much sense. We're still talking about the exact same thing. Nothing has really changed. In both situations, it's a cold winter day, there's a cabin in the woods, and a fire in the cabin. So why would they have different reactions to them? The answer, of course, is that one is a controlled environment and the other is not.

Fire!

The only change in these two scenarios is the fire. More specifically, where the fire is burning. Yet that one crucial detail either keeps our cabin warm or burns it down. This is actually a great analogy for understanding the purpose of sex. Let's say the fireplace represents marriage. It is stable, sturdy, and unmoving. It is a strong and reliable place where the "fire" of sex burns. Inside of marriage, sex takes on many more roles. It becomes warm, inviting, safe, comforting, healing, bonding, and secure. It keeps the house warm.

Outside of marriage, we don't have a strong and stable environment. There is nothing that provides the same level of commitment. Take engagements, which are a fairly strong indication of marriage. What happens if we just set our goals on being engaged when we have sex? About 60 percent of engagements don't end with marriage.[9] So that's not a great idea.

There's the idea of cohabitation, or living together before marriage. What about this option? Take a closer look, and you'll discover that most people who live together don't end up getting married. Those who do have a much higher rate of divorce. The couple is more likely to have developed a mentality that if things don't go right, they can leave or opt out, so their marriage is less likely to last during difficult times.

What about if you love your boyfriend or you feel like you're ready to have sex? Yeah, let your feelings be your guide, right?

Neither of these ideas produces good results. First, not everyone agrees on "when love happens." Even more than that, most people don't agree on when they feel ready or prepared to have sex. Some twelve-year-old boys "feel" something in their groin region that would indicate a longing for sex. Every single twelve-year-old's mother in the world would strongly disagree that this feeling means they are ready.

That brings us back, once again, to marriage. It is still the best relationship wherein both people are offered a stable and lasting environment. Outside of it, we just can't achieve the same thing.

Does this mean that sex or sexual activity isn't enticing, exciting, and inviting outside of marriage? No. I mean, there's probably a reason so many young people have sex without waiting until the best time. It's a natural desire people have, and a lot of times and for a lot of different reasons, people just have sex. I won't go into all of them, obviously. But it's also very dangerous, and a lot of people end up getting burned. It doesn't keep the house warm; instead, it usually burns it down.

How do we know this? Because high school relationships in which couples engage in sex last an average of less than four weeks. Please hear this: less than one month after teens start having sex with each other, their relationships usually end. Why does something that is so great and is supposed to bring two people together tear them apart instead?[10]

Where the fire takes place determines what purpose that fire will serve. Either it helps to keep that house warm, safe, and cozy—or it burns it down.

GIRLS ARE LOSERS

Girls, when it comes to sex, you are the losers. I wish it weren't true, but I can't find any evidence to show that it isn't. When it comes to emotions, physical risk, disease, poverty, child-bearing, child raising, and most definitely reputation, you wind up on the losing end.

If a guy sleeps with lots of girls, there is little social reaction that is deeply negative. His behavior is either praised by other guys, ignored, or talked about negatively by some females. But that's about it. People definitely don't call him a loser or write "slut" all over his locker. And if someone did say these things, he is not likely to run away bawling and then slip into an emotional depression. These words don't carry the same weight with guys. Yet if a girl sleeps with even just one guy, she might be called a slut, a tramp, or a whore. It's not fair, but it's reality.

What about the physical risks of having sex? Girls lose there too. Your reproductive system and lady parts are mostly internal. For the most part, a guy's are external. And this means that from a health and disease standpoint, girls are much more at risk when engaging in sexual activity.

Let's take a look at raising babies. It certainly starts with you. You're the one who gets pregnant, has to carry a child for nine months, and then goes through labor to have the little eight-pound ball of crying baby. Eighty percent of guys who get teenage girls pregnant do not end up parenting the child.[11] Child support is minimal, if anything. On top of that there's this stat: only one out of five teen mothers receives any financial support from her child's father at all.[12] Check the food and diaper section at any store, and you'll find that these things don't come cheap. In fact, about 75 percent of teen moms will live under the poverty line for most of their lives.[13] Their children are three times more likely to live in poverty as well.

OTHER NOT AWESOME STUFF

- Seventy percent of teen mothers drop out of high school, making pregnancy the primary reason young women drop out early. Only 30 percent of teen mothers complete high school by age 30, compared to 76 percent of women who delay parenthood until age 21 or older.
- Teen marriages are twice as likely to end in divorce as marriages in which the woman is at least 25 years old.
- Nearly 80 percent of fathers of children born to teen mothers do not marry the mothers.[14]

//////////////// WARNING! ////////////////

A teenager gets pregnant every forty-two seconds in this country.[15] Almost anyone would say that's entirely too many pregnancies. And while this is a tragedy, it is a reality that needs some tenderness. These are people who have hearts and deserve love and dignity. Single moms need plenty of encouragement, and they deserve lots of hugs. But there's also something to learn from this subject. Choose ahead of time not to face any of this stuff to begin with. It's not about just getting by in life; it's about learning how to soar in this life of yours.

//

EMOTIONAL STUFF

The neglected part of the sex subject is the stuff that happens to the heart. The emotional aspect. It's the subject guys don't think about much, and it's all girls want to talk about. Seriously. They talk about this on a steroidal level. So what happens with your emotions when you choose to have sex prematurely, outside of marriage? For starters, and as you might expect by now, sex affects guys and girls in pretty different ways, at least initially. When it comes to feelings of attachment, which are somewhat chemical, guys don't feel the same way at this point in their lives. A girl's teenage brain, feelings, and emotions are much more connected than a guy's.

When a girl has sex, she thinks about what happened, talks about it with her friends, and writes about it, or just continues to reflect on it, which means it affects her constantly. Now given that, on average, teens in this type of relationship usually break up within a few weeks after sex, she loses again. Oh, and for those people justifying their great relationship by saying "My boyfriend loves me; we had sex three months ago and we're still together," I'm sorry, but the overall physical, psychological, mental, social, and even spiritual health of a sexually active, unwed person tends to decline. In other words, sex does not make you happier or feel more loved. On average, grades go down, pregnancy and disease go up, and emotional health and self-esteem decline compared to someone who isn't engaging in extramarital sexual activity. The evidence is overwhelming.

Here is the important part. Despite all of this, you need guys and guys still need you. I mean, who do guys want to marry? Girls! With that said, if you lose, then guys lose too. We're all in this together. It's important for us to respect one another. We are on the same team, after all. Likewise, and equally important, it's critical that you respect yourself, your body, your heart, your relationships, and your friendships with guys. Just think how much nicer it would be if you didn't have to worry so much about any negative consequences in your relationships. After all, relationships are *meant* to be good.

/////////////// WARNING! ///////////////

When you have sex with someone and that relationship ends, it doesn't really end. Sex is emotional and physical. It isn't just something people do. It has major effects. It just does. There is oxytocin, vasopressin, and all kinds of chemicals that our bodies produce that change us and create bonds and change our emotions. Also babies and stuff. And when relationships and sex end, people take all that junk from one relationship right into the next. Fear, hurt, jealousy, insecurity, disease, and anything else that is a part of you doesn't just go away. It usually gets passed on to the next relationship, and the next, and the one after that. And to be honest, that sounds pretty awful. Sex is meant to bond people, and bonding with the right person is pretty important, to say the least. Planning sex at the right time—in the safety of marriage—will keep you from having life-changing regrets.

Sex is incredibly beautiful and poetic and magnetic and completing. But only if you will let it be. I sure hope you will.

///

NEWS FLASH!

The biggest message in all of this is to understand the natural progression that relationships should take—from dating to love to marriage to sex. Sex is no substitute for the earlier steps in that progression. Sex can seal, enhance, strengthen, and bond love together. But sex can never be great if love and commitment are not solidly in place to begin with.

⟶ DISCUSSION STUFF ⟵

1. What are the three most common messages that you hear about sex today? What effect, if any, do you think this has on you?
2. Why would people pass off sex as something casual and something that's not a big deal? Do these people/companies/ messages have your best interest at heart, or something else?
3. If sex is supposed to bring people closer, why do most teenagers in relationships break up shortly after having sex?
4. Do you think girls or guys are more negatively affected by sex? Why?

5. Does the analogy of the "cabin in the woods" help explain the importance of when and how sex happens?
6. What is something that you need to understand better about sex, the physical act of love, and the thing that makes babies? Is there a trusted adult you could turn to for information?

chapter 18

THE THING ABOUT LOVE

{
Gravitation cannot be held
responsible for people falling in love.
—Albert Einstein
}

If there is one thing I am certain of, it's that I don't understand love. I mean, I'm not sure any one person will ever understand even half of what love is. We pretty much base our lives around love, getting it and giving it. For thousands of years, we have written about it, tried to define it, sell it, put it in different categories, and have searched desperately for it.

I do know this: Love to me now is not what it was five years ago, and it won't be the same five years from now. In fact, it's always changing and, hopefully, growing.

Romantic love is the part that is constantly being thrown

> Once in a while, in the middle of an ordinary life, love gives us a fairy tale
>
> —Unknown

at us. But it is also only one small part of love. Sometimes there are tiny little snippets, memories, or pictures that pop up in my head that also seem to have love written all over them:

♡ a mother looking at her child
♡ seeing my favorite artist play the piano and sing
♡ seeing a father hug his son
♡ two friends looking out from the top of a mountain peak
♡ any picture of Mother Teresa
♡ the love and pride my soldier friend has for his country
♡ the whole Bible

And you know what? The more I look, the more I see that love is actually everywhere. And sometimes we make it so small.

SHHH!

I'll tell you what a lot of guys would love to hear a girl say. And you didn't hear this from me:

Imagine that a guy is standing there with the girl of his dreams . . . you. And that both of you are now beyond being teenagers. He's a great guy: honest, loving, confident, and committed. I'll bet that he would love nothing more than to hear you say something like this: "I have thought about you for so long.

I may not have known you or seen you, but you have always been in my heart. As I grew up and had other relationships, I have been planning for you. In all the decisions about my heart, I protected it. I did it so that I would know how to love you and be loved by you."

I mean, I'm just putting together a scenario here, but if a girl ever said something like that to me, I would probably start crying. I mean, do push-ups. Or cry. Even if guys don't act like this stuff is important, it is. Guys want a girl who knows two things. First, that she is really valuable. Second, that she thinks he is really valuable too.

GUY TIP

I wouldn't exactly say this on the first date. Or the ninth either. (It might really freak him out.) Just know that if you do choose to think about these things ahead of time, and to live your life with these things in mind, it will shine through in everything you do and say along the way. And it will affect the outcome. In a big, huge, wonderful way, I might add.

GUYS WANT TO BE WANTED

Underneath many of the things we've been talking about, there's something more, something stronger and deeper in a guy's psyche. Sure, guys talk a lot about sex and girls and games and farting and other somewhat trivial dumb stuff. There is one thing, though, that is the real driving force behind why we guys act the way we do. It's the need to be wanted.

NEWS FLASH!

In surveys about guys' sexual desires, three out of four guys said that if they had all the sex they wanted, they would still be unsatisfied.

Guys need validation and acceptance of who they are just like you do. Guys need someone to let them know that they are okay just the way they are. And when it comes to love from a girl one day, that's what a guy wants too . . . to show love to a girl and to be loved in return. In a lot of ways, guys aren't that different from you at the core. Sometimes it's a matter of finding the right time, place, and, more important, the right person to share love with.

So be careful along the way. And here are some "don'ts" for you:

- Don't let yourself get taken in by the wrong guy.
- Don't listen to what people say more than what they do.
- Don't let the gift of sex become something cheap.
- Don't allow yourself to be used, pressured, or intimidated.
- Don't think of love as just something that's about romance.

Things Treasured

Sometimes I think we settle for playing with mud when God has promised us gold. Well, God wants you to put down that mud and trust him. He wants you to understand that he has a treasure waiting for you. And the more I understand God, the more I think he wants everyone—guys and girls—to focus on the heart, and not on the body. A friend of mine always says, "A girl's heart and body should be so wrapped up in God that a man has to go directly to him to ask for it."

And wouldn't that be nice? A guy who asks for directions?

Whenever I'm not sure what love is, I read this slowly and find that it answers all of my questions about my tiny version of love:

Love is patient and kind. Love is not jealous, it does not brag, and it is not proud. Love is not rude, is not selfish, and does not get upset with others. Love does not count up wrongs that have been done. Love takes no pleasure in evil but rejoices over the truth. Love patiently accepts all things. It always trusts, always hopes, and always endures. Love never ends.
—1 Corinthians 13:4-8

---------------→ DISCUSSION STUFF ←---------------

1. Give your best definition of love. (And not one found in a forwarded e-mail full of cute puppies and rainbows.)
2. Are there ways in which you have limited your definition of love? How so?
3. How does restricting love to "romantic love" limit the word?
4. What fears do you think guys experience when it comes to the idea of love?
5. How do you know if what you are experiencing is really love? Compare it to what 1 Corinthians 13:4–8 says about love.

ROAD TRIP

{ It is one of the blessings of old friends that you can afford to be stupid with them. }

—Ralph Waldo Emerson

{ Real friends are those who, when you feel you've made a fool of yourself, don't feel you've done a permanent job. }

—Anonymous

GUY SUPERGLUE

A lot of people have opinions about how connected things are for girls in life. Which can beg the question, "How do guys bond?" I've been asked this question again and again. The easiest answer is this: "Road trip!"

Fundamental differences: Guys bond differently in the sense that we connect from the experiences we share together. Girls bond more from the emotions they share with one another.

OUR COMFORT ZONE

Guys don't tend to sit around sharing all our feelings about a tough emotional week. It's just not our choice way to talk. We need a comfortable—emphasis on *comfortable*—place to let down our guard. We might play tough, but when it comes to opening up, guys are delicate little daisies.

"Did you go pee in the adult diaper yet? Does it feel weird? Is it awesome?"

—One of many quotes between my friends and me while road tripping

For example, when I was in college, summer break rolled around in May, and I had a couple of weeks free between my summer classes and heading out to work at a summer camp. Even better, my two best friends had free time too. It didn't take us long to figure out how to use our time. It just clicked: "Road trip!" And just like that, it was on.

RIDICULOUSNESS

We headed out in an old Honda, just the three of us—Ryan, Luke, and myself—ready for absolutely anything, including what we weren't ready for. In just over a week, we made our way from Oxford, Ohio, up the coast of the Great Lakes, through Pennsylvania, to a cottage in New York. From there we planned on hitting Niagara Falls, Canada, Vermont, New Hampshire, Connecticut, New York City, Boston, Philadelphia, and Columbus before heading back to our school. I'm still pretty proud of this list, by the way.

We had a huge list of things to do, and the driving force was the adventure into the unknown. We drove almost two thousand miles, camped out on a beach, got into some mischief, slept in weird places, ate some pretty weird food, and not once—not one single time—did we listen to the radio.

{ Deep experience is never peaceful.
—Henry James }

I probably learned more about my friends in that week than I did the two years before that. That's what a road trip does. It gives guys a proper setting in which to bond. Why? Because we were sitting next to each other, looking at stuff, going places, and it just sort of . . . happened. It happened in a very comfortable way. It was an adventure, something we could experience and accomplish, and it brought us together in the process.

On the Road Again . . .

I remember a lot about that trip. I don't know about your run-of-the-mill weeks, but some of mine come and go without me even noticing. But during that week, I saw the beautiful New York countryside on Lake Erie. I sat in an awesome cottage in a tiny and forgotten little town. I ate unusual foods, sat around a campfire, and played on the beach. As a joke, we posed on a beached sailboat, and it actually ended up as a pretty great photo of me with my friends. Later, I had the picture made into a painting for my friend when he got married. It still hangs in his living room.

We stared at Niagara Falls and hiked around them for hours. We climbed down a ledge of the cliffs and had someone very, very quickly take our picture on the edge before getting chased off.

We talked our way into the kitchen at a famous restaurant where buffalo wings were invented. Suddenly we were in the kitchen making the wings with the cooks, mixing the sauce, and tossing them into the air and spilling them everywhere. We talked for nine straight hours as we headed up to Dartmouth, made a handful of friends on campus, walked the historic river, made clay pottery, and went hiking and camping in the New Hampshire mountains. We looked at a bunch of stores dedicated to the works of Dr. Seuss (who went to Dartmouth), played music in the courtyards with some guys we met, and then drove to some little towns in Massachusetts.

We saw where they filmed a bunch of movies about the ocean and fishing, and then we visited a two-hundred-year-old fishing tavern and ate clam chowder while overlooking the ocean. We walked around Harvard, looked at museums, and talked in our worst Boston accents. We listened to subway musicians and sat in on some great jazz. We went to MIT and snuck into the classroom where they filmed *Good Will Hunting* and wrote funny things on the boards, took our picture, and then ran away. We tossed a Frisbee and casually talked about nuclear physics with the students sitting on the lawns at MIT. (Mostly we just nodded.) We took in the sights, sounds, and smells of New York City. We watched a guy dance in the subway, walked through Times Square, ate hot dogs, and got ripped off by street vendors when we bought "designer" watches that broke a couple of weeks later. (P.S. It was not a good deal, Luke. I hope you can see that now.) And we took in a lot of Korean customs with Luke's grandparents in the city.

We were sleep-deprived and ready to go home by the end of the week. But we'd also had the best time of our lives. It was the most intense road trip I've ever taken, and it was awesome.

Don't get me wrong, I'm sure that both guys and girls like road trips. They are fun, and you can act really dumb and it makes them even better. But that's not the point. For guys, it's the experience that bonds us together. It provides a backdrop for "bonding" to take place.

▷ DISCUSSION STUFF ◁

---

1. Name five of the best ways that girls bond.
2. Now name five ways that you think guys bond best. Is there any overlap?
3. Why do you think we need to bond with people? Where does that need come from?
4. Does talking or sharing experiences help you feel closer to people? Why?
5. If you could go on a trip anywhere in the world for a month, where would you go? Why? Who would you take with you? Come on—dream a little!

chapter 20

PRESSURE

{ When we long for life without
difficulties, remind us that oaks
grow strong in contrary winds
and diamonds are made under
pressure. }

—Peter Marshall

TURN THE SWITCH OFF

There's a huge pressure switch you have to control. It has settings like "popular culture" and "the going thing." It's powerful and can have a profound effect on your life. It's also a huge joke. Sure, we make fun of past trends, but all the while, we're religiously following the newest ones. And that means that if there is some sort of joke, then it is usually on us. But the good news is that you can have control over a lot of it.

The people who try to sell you everything from T-shirts to entire lifestyles put tremendous pressure on both girls and guys every day. It affects your clothes, the latest clever sayings, what you watch on TV, which websites you frequent, the music you listen to, where you vacation, and what you will name your future kids. There are diet trends, makeup lines, fashion statements, electronic gadgets everyone has to have, and the list never stops. And you know what? Sometimes all that I hear in life is just . . . noise.

Do yourself a favor. Stop. Really, just stop. Take a deep breath, and be still. Now, if you didn't, I hope you will read it again and do it this time. Sometimes we have to pause and turn the noise off.

I've never felt better about myself by being the way other people tell me to be. And it is weird that I've spent so much time listening to them. The truth is, most of these ideas about how you should be are a waste of your very valuable time. They come and go with the tides and spring fashion trends, and meanwhile they keep you from finding your deeper identity, which usually isn't on a shirt.

GUY TIP

Finding your own identity is more attractive to guys— especially the right guys.

I recently read a book that talked about getting rid of distractions. The president of a large university read an article that concluded that after a twenty-four-hour day, 99 percent of the articles and daily things people spend their time reading would never be read again.[1] Essentially, the things we take up a lot of our time with have a tiny shelf life.

So he decided to do an interesting experiment. He cut everything out of his life that he could for a six-month period of time. He stopped sending e-mails, reading the paper, and watching TV. He even stopped listening to the radio, surfing the Web, and talking on the phone—except when absolutely necessary. His conclusion was interesting. He summarized what he missed out on was this: *nothing!* He didn't miss a single thing.

All of these things that seem so important are often just distractions. I thought it was interesting that in this story the university president came to the conclusion that he resented a lot of the things he had gotten used to before. Sometimes it feels as if people are constantly invading our thoughts and life without our permission.

JUUUUUST A THOUGHT

Have you ever thought about tuning out the constant messages in life that you're being told to obsess about, like guys, your appearance, and all that trendy stuff that never ends? Does it ever make you mad when you think about all of these people telling you who you need to be or dress like or be obsessed with? It makes me mad, because I want to be in charge of my life. I don't want to feel like a little monkey who dances and sings when he's told to. And you know what? I love monkeys, especially the little ones. But I don't want to be one.

What are some of the extra things that you feel you must have every day? Can you identify the stuff that takes up a ton of your time and you can live without? Hint: if you do them every day, you probably feel like you can't live without them. (Obviously not breathing, school, speaking languages, or going to the bathroom.) Look at stuff like using the computer, the phone, television, car, and so on.

If you are brave, try cutting out all these extra things for one week. Just do it. Don't think about it or reason with yourself. Take a break from the monkey show. Stop e-mailing. Who cares if you don't e-mail or instant-message or get on Facebook for a week? You can get back to it, and you probably won't have missed out on anything too dramatic in life.

Give yourself the freedom to take a test run. It's only one week. You'll probably come up with some interesting conclusions. There is one that will be evident very quickly: you are not missing out on the stuff you were afraid of missing out on. Sometimes all those things can block your focus on the stuff that does make a real difference in your life.

Making a choice to weed out distractions at this point in your life can have a significant impact on you and your future. It can open fresh new doors to self-discovery that you may not have ever experienced before. It can make your life less stressful. It will allow you to be yourself, to make friends with people who like you for who you are, and perhaps eventually to attract a guy who will also appreciate these things.

SHHH!

Getting rid of distractions is all part of the filtering system that helps you find the real you. Also, it's easier for the right person to find you. You'll learn to identify and avoid unnecessary distractions, which will allow you to enjoy a much better life.

THE INTERNET

All of the world's information is at our fingertips, and mostly we just look at nonsensical Internet thingies.

Girls, here is a little Internet information as it relates to guys. It can be an easy way for guys to learn about you with little or no effort. Meaning, the more boundaries around you there are, the more people actually have to come *to you* to learn about you. Plus, the Internet and the real world are two completely different places. One is easily accessible and there's nothing to lose; the other is a big gamble and takes risk and confidence.

The Internet can be a pretty weird place. I think it also enables us to form some strange habits. For example, if there is something we don't like, we just click out of it and make it disappear, so it always leaves us in control. If I don't like what someone says, I just click good-bye. No conflict resolution lessons on the Internet. Ya know, stuff like that is kind of weird.

The Internet is also pretty unfiltered and therefore by nature strange and even dangerous. Parents have to set up blocks ahead of time to make sure no porn or "adult" weird content ever comes looking for you. That represents a pretty significant shift in culture, by the way: you used to have to go out of your way to look for all the bad stuff in life; but now, it comes looking for you.

When it comes to guys, the whole Internet thing means that they can take risks that aren't really risks at all. It is easier, after all, to have a lot of confidence sitting in a room behind a computer screen. But people face-to-face are different. They aren't screens or mouse clicks or profile pages.

Simple Rules of Thumb

Here are a couple of recommendations for you. Don't ever let a guy ask you a question on the computer, in a text, or on the phone that he wouldn't ask you in person. If you allow this, then you are giving him the easy way out. Make it harder than that. Don't be so available, and don't be at his beck and call. It will come back to bite you in the long run, and you'll be robbing a guy of the confidence muscles he will need in life.

Make a guy who likes you put on his parachute, take a deep breath, walk to the edge of the cliff, and jump off. Let him show he's willing to risk rejection in order to spend time with you. If he can't, then he isn't ready or willing, and neither of those things is your problem. Shortcuts with people are cheating, and it hurts everyone in the long run.

→ Discussion Stuff ←

---

1. What are the greatest pressures in your life? Who put them there—you, or someone or something else?
2. Where does the "noise" come from in your life?
3. Is there some of that "noise" that you could cut out of your life for a week? List those things, and then do it. What changes did you experience from cutting those things out?

4. How much time do you spend "social networking"? What could you do with that time instead?

5. Are there ways in which the identity that you are forming, partially from outside influences, might be stopping you from attracting positive things and people in your life? How so?

6. What is a new hobby, passion, or endeavor you have wanted to start that you have felt you didn't have time for? What could help you make time for it?

1   2   3   (4)

I Have Some Questions

{
Happy is the person who finds
wisdom, the one who gets
understanding.

—Proverbs 3:13
}

chapter 21

SERIOUSLY? YOU HAVE MORE QUESTIONS?

This is my wish for you:
Comfort on difficult days,
smiles when sadness intrudes,
rainbows to follow the clouds,
laughter to kiss your lips,
sunsets to warm your heart,
hugs when spirits sag,
beauty for your eyes to see,
friendships to brighten your being,
faith so that you can believe,
confidence for when you doubt,
courage to know yourself,
patience to accept the truth,
love to complete your life.
—Anonymous

ALSO THERE'S MORE STUFF

I know this book hasn't addressed every issue you face in life, or even close to it, but this is just one book, after all. I thought I would also include some of the most common questions girls ask me about guys. And . . . well, maybe a few other things.

Q: Do fish sleep?

A: Um . . . I don't know, and honestly, I don't care too much. I think some of them might. I know dolphins only shut down half of their brain at a time to sleep. I'll have to look into it with the fishes. So I guess we should move on to other questions that aren't marine life–based in nature . . .

• • • • • • • • • • • • • Dating • • • • • • • • • • • • •

Q: How do you know what your boundaries should be with someone you are dating?

A: That's a great question. There are lots of different answers and opinions. The answers vary quite a bit, but I'll try to simplify it with one thought. It's the best rule I've ever heard and actually makes sense. Don't do anything in private that you aren't okay doing in public.

If you think about it, this one can be a pretty good guideline. Bring your conscience into play when it comes to the limits. If you have nothing to hide, you're free to get to know one another. It keeps you from having to be sneaky, question your decisions, and defend the stuff you're doing.

The second rule of thumb with boundaries is to keep your bodies in an upright position when you are together. When the two of you decide to go horizontal, it automatically makes people think about the stuff people do when they lie down with each other. Staying upright is both good for your posture and for your self-respect. Double win, ya know?

• • • • • • •   The Guy Superiority Factor   • • • • • • •

Q: Guys can be real snobs. Why do they assume you have a crush on them if you smile at them more than once?

A: Overcompensation, my friend. And somewhat normal for young peeps. Guys look for ego boosts to assure self-confidence. If there are guys acting like this, there are a couple of things you can do: (1) let them be, and (2) be nice and go on your way.

Seriously, this isn't something that you are going to fix. People's hearts go through renovations at different times. I would leave that one to God. The point for you is that a guy is probably not going to be a good friend or boyfriend if he is too caught up in himself. It's also not your problem, and you should find other ways to fill your time.

• • • • • • • • Guys Can Be Possessive • • • • • • • •

Q: Guys want to have their cake and eat it too. They give their girlfriends a hard time about talking to other guys, so why is it okay for them to continue flirting?

A: In some cases, I'm sure you are right. If some guys had their way, they would probably stamp "Mine!" all over every girl they wanted to date or had an interest in. But that's not all guys either. When guys are overly possessive, it shows a lack of confidence. Don't buy into any other explanations. Being possessive is selfish and it's wrong, whether or not it's being done by a guy or a girl. Plus, it's also not real. No one can possess anyone else, so it's weird to behave as if you can. It's also a sign that one (or both) of you doesn't have the maturity to be dating anyone just yet.

If a guy is acting that way, it's a telltale sign that he still has a lot of growing up to do. If he is insecure because you really are flirting and sending mixed signals, then . . . stop it. And that part is on you. This is also a sign you aren't mature enough to be in a relationship yet. In essence, maturity and time help with a lot of these things. I know you love that answer.

• • • • • • • • Is This the Real Thing? • • • • • • • •

Q: I have been dating my boyfriend for a long time,

and I really feel like he is the one. Is there a good way to know if this is for real?

A: Well . . . I don't know you or your boyfriend. But I'll do my best to take a stab at this one.

Are feelings your only measure of reality? If they are, start adjusting now, because otherwise your life will be a confusing roller coaster. Also, I think it's smart for a girl to be overcautious as opposed to under-cautious and naive. Only a few guys in their teens are thinking about marriage.

If you think, *This is true love; we will be together forever, no matter what people say,* consider this: more than 96 percent of high school relationships don't last, including ones that were "absolutely going to be together forever." So it's a good idea not to make any assumptions just yet. Knowing the facts can protect you from making some bad decisions. If I sound unromantic, I'm sorry.

Truth first, romance later. The truth is, you will probably date several guys before you get married, so treat each one with care. Learn from each experience and relationship. Don't look at every relationship as if you are going to wind up getting married. Deal with the facts before you let your feelings take over. Remember, protect your heart, even from your own feelings when you need to. I recommend enjoying real friendships while you are in high school. You learn just as much, and I can't think of any downsides to that.

• • • • • • • •   Guys Are Pushy About Sex   • • • • • • • •

Q: My boyfriend is really pushy about messing around, and I feel a lot of pressure to have sex or do other physical things with him. I have a hard time saying no because I don't want to make him mad, and I really love him.

A: Wow. There are too many girls in situations like this. Guys sometimes, girls most times. First, get out of the relationship right now. You don't have the self-control, self-respect, maturity, or self-confidence you need. One out of four girls is sexually molested in some way during her life.[1] Countless others get put into situations that they don't know what to do about, and they wind up doing things they regret.

Saying no is a very important part of any relationship. It's actually very important in general. If you don't learn to say no, life will be much harder. You can never please everyone, so stop trying—like yesterday, already. Protect yourself first, and then care for others, in that order. You must come first in this equation. Don't be in a relationship that has pressure; it means someone is getting hurt. Healthy relationships are about patience and encouragement and friendship—not pressure.

If you find yourself in a high-pressure situation, try this sarcastic response. Say, "Let me talk to my parents about it first." Then pick up your cell phone and call your mom and dad. When they answer the phone, tell them your date wants to have sex with you, and he'd like their permission to do that, in addition to possibly getting you pregnant, assuming responsibility for the child, taking care of the medical bills, vowing to be there when you feel bloated, and attending most family functions. See if he's on board after this. And keep in mind the following response as a jumping-off point:

GUY: I want to do this with you. If you love me you would too.

GIRL: Oh, that's weird. I thought if you loved me then you would consider not manipulating me. And maybe respecting how I feel. I guess we're both wrong.

Sex does not make love. **Period.**

••• Guys Think Complimenting Girls Isn't Cool •••

Q: All my girlfriends say I look pretty, but even when I make a huge effort and look my best, no guys ever even seem to notice.

A: That is difficult, I'm sure. It's nice when people compliment us. But here's another simple answer: don't try to dress up and go looking for compliments. Sometimes that subconscious motive shows, and it

rubs people the wrong way. Whenever I meet someone who is craving attention, it usually pushes me
away instantly.

While it's nice to receive compliments, they will not
and should not create your self-worth, so don't expect
them to. You'll be let down if you let other people
determine your worth and beauty.

• • • • • • Guys Never Make a Commitment • • • • • •

Q: Why do some guys suddenly withdraw from a relationship and say they don't want to be tied down?

A: Simply put, it's called *fight-or-flight*. It's built in as a
defensive strategy. When you are in an uneasy situation
like being chased by a tiger or being uncertain how you
feel about a girl, you often get hit by feelings of either
(1) approaching potential conflict, or (2) avoiding it and
running away. Guess which one is usually easier?

Oftentimes, a guy just isn't ready to be in a deep,
committed relationship when he is young, and only
when he gets into it does he realize this. Not all guys
feel that way, but as teenagers, there is nothing wrong
with a guy not wanting a relationship. Some of it is natural. Not easy, but natural. The annoying part is when a
guy leads a girl on, makes promises, or pursues someone he then backs out on. The good news is that if you
protect yourself and use friendship as the long-term
guide, you don't have to worry about getting hurt.

Remember, it's up to you to protect yourself. In these situations, time is a great tool and probably the easiest to use. I think friendship is a pretty good filter to see things through. But that's just me . . . silly old friendship guy. Also, building friendships prepares you for a good marriage relationship later.

• • • • • • • • • • Guys Are Insensitive • • • • • • • • • •

Q: Why do guys seem so insensitive to girls' feelings?

A: If you haven't figured this out by now, let me remind you: guys are different creatures. Our sensitivity will change over time as we grow up. Girls are more emotionally aware at younger ages, and they are capable of expressing their thoughts and feelings better. Make friends, not boyfriends, and this stuff will work itself out. Don't force things until the right time.

• • • Guys Think Fighting Shows Their Strength • • •

Q: I can't stand it when guys try to show how tough they are and how big their muscles are. Why do they try to act so macho?

A: *What, these arms? Uhhh . . . honestly, I thought I left them in the garage. I don't even normally bring these guys.*
It seems funny to girls, but guys acting tough or macho is also normal, to a degree. At some point in the

teenage years, guys naturally realize their desire to feel strong. So they try and get that strength and then show off that strength. Strength and confidence usually go hand in hand. We are simply trying to say "I want to be strong, and I guess maybe this will build some confidence."

The truth is, a guy needs a great example of strength in his life. Both to help him build his strength and to teach him that it takes strength to show kindness and compassion. If guys don't have an example (and many don't), they usually resort to acting in some ridiculous way.

• • • • • • • • • • • Puzzle Pieces • • • • • • • • • • •

Q: If most guy/girl relationships don't last, what's a good way to have a relationship in high school? Is there any answer?

A: There are some really good ways to think about this. Especially if you think about this whole thing as a learning experience. You are learning, both what you want and need, and what you don't want or need. Life's full of adventures to learn from. How you start your relationships will impact the way you end them. This can be good or bad news. That's up to you. If you start things out as friends, you may leave things that way too. Generally speaking, if you start out with romance immediately, the flame dies out quickly, and you are left without feelings of deep care or friendship.

Friendship is a good answer to a lot of the problems that girls and guys encounter. If you're friends, then you kind of start with, "I care about you and your well-being." That says a lot in itself.

You don't just represent yourself in your relationships. You represent your family, your morals, your beliefs, and depending where you are with it, your faith as well. Strive to represent them with the love and respect they deserve.

→ Discussion Stuff ←

1. What is a dating boundary you can create that will help you specifically? Why?
2. Sometimes guys overcompensate with things like muscles, aggression, cars, and gadgets. But girls sometimes overcompensate too. Are there ways that you might be overcompensating? Come on . . . be honest.
3. How would you evaluate whether or not your relationship with a guy is "the real thing"? Would your standards be the same five years from now? How might they be different?
4. Are you comfortable saying no, and have you? How might this affect you in a dating scenario?
5. Do you crave attention from guys in ways that could be unhealthy? What are they?
6. How do you think the fight-or-flight response can affect both guys and girls when it comes to dating and relationships?

7. Describe a time you saw a guy acting really macho. What did his posture look like? What was he doing or saying? How was his voice different? Now . . . why might he have been acting this way?

8. If you replaced the idea of love and dating and romance with the idea of deep friendship, what are the drawbacks and benefits you think you might experience? Why?

chapter 22

ON THE WAY OUT . . .

Sometimes I get overzealous and dumb. I want to approach every single topic you'd ever have to deal with as a teen, so you'd understand things better in every circumstance that comes up in life. But then I'd end up with a ten-thousand-page book that probably nobody would read. Sometimes we have to have a little patience—in writing, in relationships, with God, and perhaps with principles that promise to pay off.

It's been quite a process for me. Especially the part where I try to understand how God fits into all of these equations. The funny part is that I was usually thinking about it backward. I find that he gives me a lot of evidence that he is the designer of these equations.

SANTA ON STEROIDS

When I was a kid, I spent a lot of time on this "being cool" thing. I dunno why now, but it seemed like a pretty strong current moving the river I was in at the time. I believed in God and thought Jesus seemed important enough to draw pictures of, but he didn't do much for me. Jesus never stopped kids from making fun of me at school. He wasn't someone I could eat lunch with, and he never helped me with my homework. He didn't make my family loving and whole.

The whole idea of God being love and truth never seemed to translate from the Bible into real life. I needed people to like me, I needed to fit in, and I needed to know that I had value. I mean, at some point, you want to think that your existence has some actual value, ya know?

When I wound up in a juvenile detention center and then rehab by age fifteen, I realized my plan wasn't working. I wasn't fitting in, I was saying all the wrong things, I was angry, and none of the girls I wanted to like me ever did. There was obviously something wrong with me. I knew I wanted something better, but I didn't know what that was or how to get it.

Life's answers sure do come from the most unexpected places sometimes. For me . . . most times. The people in that rehabilitation center gave me something very valuable: hope—hope that things could be different. I started to realize that I wasn't a piece of junk, and that feelings aren't always an indicator of truth. Sometimes feelings actually lie to me, and that makes me feel funny about feelings, actually.

Then I realized how much Jesus was always telling people about these things like hope and forgiveness and love. For the first time in my life, these promises seemed to make sense. Like

> What we are is God's gift to us. What we become is our gift to God.
>
> —Eleanor Powell

they were the answers for things that we all need, if we are honest with ourselves.

I realized I had been thinking of God as Santa Claus on steroids, monitoring my "naughty or nice" progress. I began to see that God constantly shows his love to people throughout the course of time. He said things that make sense today, like care about people the way you want them to care about you. He also said not to steal, and to forgive people who wrong us. And when I think about the things he said, and why he said them, they really make sense. The compassion that Jesus had really was unique. And I liked him. I realized that if he were standing in front of me saying the weird little parables about fishing and doing miracles where people were blind and then saw, I would probably drop what I was doing to follow him too. I didn't become a perfect Christian. That would be impossible since Jesus Christ is the only person without a single transgression.

I still wanted to fit in, be good at sports, and get girls to like me. But it seemed different when I actually let God's principles guide me. I realized that when I tried to see things through Jesus' eyes, I became a better friend to everyone else.

KEEP YOUR HEAD UP

This is where you come in. When I think back to that time when I was fifteen and alone, there was one critical thing missing in my life—actually knowing that I was valuable. I just couldn't see it. I had believed a bunch of mixed messages and lies about who I was and who I wasn't. And I hope you will not do that.

You have a lot to learn, and it takes time. You'll trip up now and then, do something dumb, be mean, or not value yourself. What I mean is . . . keep learning. Keep loving people. Keep getting better—to others and to yourself. Keep your head up and keep going forward. But know this. You do belong! You are valuable! I mean that with all of my heart.

There is no other you. Things that are unique and valuable have another name . . . we call them treasures. And you are a unique and valuable treasure made by God.

I hope and I pray that you will see yourself the way God sees you. I hope you see your great qualities and your value for just being you. Because when this happens, it's a lot easier for other people to see how great you are too.

All the best as you keep on this journey of yours. Keep me up to date.

chapter **23**

TRUE BUT SLIGHTLY UN-AWESOME THINGS

TEEN PREGNANCY

- ✧ More than 750,000 teen girls get pregnant every year.[1]
- ✧ The United States has the highest rates of teen pregnancy, birth, and abortion in the industrialized world.[2]
- ✧ Approximately three in ten girls will become pregnant in the United States at least once before the age of twenty.[3]
- ✧ Children of teens are more likely to do poorly in school, more likely to drop out of school, and less likely to attend college.[4]
- ✧ Nearly 80 percent of teen boys who father children do not marry the mother of their child and pay less than $800 annually in child support.[5]
- ✧ Nearly 40 percent of the fathers of children born to teen mothers are age twenty or older.[6]

◇ Every year, there are approximately 15 million new cases of STDs (forty-one thousand per day; eight thousand of those are teens).[7]

◇ Approximately one in four sexually active teens is infected with an STD.[8]

◇ In the 1960s, only syphilis and gonorrhea were common. Today there are at least fifty STDs, and at least eight new pathogens have been identified since 1980, including HIV.[9]

◇ Less than half of adults ages eighteen to forty-four have ever been tested for an STD other than HIV/AIDS.[10]

◇ At least 15 percent of all infertile American women are infertile because of tubal damage caused by pelvic inflammatory disease (PID), the result of an untreated STD.[11]

◇ It is estimated that as many as one in four Americans has genital herpes, yet at least 80 percent of those with herpes are unaware they have it.[12]

◇ Two-thirds of all STDs occur in people age twenty-five or younger.[13]

DRUGS, SEX, AND ALCOHOL

✳ Teens fifteen and older who drink are seven times likelier to have sexual intercourse and twice as likely to have it with four or more partners as nondrinking teens.[14]

✳ Teens fourteen and younger who use drugs are four times likelier to have sex than those who don't.[15]

* Teens fourteen and younger who use alcohol are twice as likely to have sex as those who don't.[16]
* About 75 percent of the men and at least 55 percent of the women involved in acquaintance rapes had been drinking or taking drugs just before the attack.[17]
* Sixty-three percent of teens who use alcohol and 70 percent of teens who are frequent drinkers have had sex, compared to 26 percent of those who never drink.[18]
* Seventy-two percent of teens who use drugs and 81 percent of those who use them heavily have had sex, compared to 36 percent of those who never use drugs.[19]
* Teens fifteen and older who use drugs are five times likelier to have sexual intercourse and three times likelier to have it with four or more partners than those who don't.[20]

RAPE

» One out of four girls and one out of six boys are sexually abused before age eighteen.[21]
» Eighty-six percent of rapes are committed by someone the victim knows.[22]
» Seventy-eight percent of teen rape victims do not tell their parents that they have been raped.[23]
» Forty-two percent of assaults happen in the victim's own home.[24]
» About 75 percent of the men and at least 55 percent of the women involved in acquaintance rapes had been drinking or taking drugs just before the attack.[25]

» Girls who are sexually abused often suffer from a traumatic and profound lack of self-esteem. These girls engage in disempowering and self-defeating behaviors, which can propel them into a cycle of prostitution, addiction, drug dealing, and violence.[26]

» Thirty-eight percent of date rape survivors are females between the ages of fourteen and seventeen.[27]

» Child sexual abuse is more frequent within families than outside families; disabled children are especially at risk of sexual abuse, especially from people they already know.[28]

» The average age for the onset of a sexually abusive relationship is six to eight years old.[29]

» Fifty-seven percent of rapes occur while out on a date.[30]

» In 2003, 83 percent of the episodes of the top twenty shows among teen viewers contained some sexual content, including 20 percent with sexual intercourse.[31]

» Sixty-two percent of teen rapes are perpetrated by classmates or friends.[32]

» More than 70 percent of girls in the juvenile justice system or in shelters have histories of sexual abuse or assault.[33]

» One in four sexual assaults takes place in the victim's home, making it the most common place for a sexual assault to take place. Three out of five sexual assaults occur at night, with the largest proportion occurring between 6:00 p.m. and midnight.[34]

» On average, music videos contain ninety sexual situations per hour, including eleven "hard-core" scenes depicting behaviors such as intercourse and oral sex.[35]

» Seventy-five percent of women raped are between the ages of fifteen and twenty-one. The average age is eighteen.[36]

» Girls who watch more than fourteen hours of rap music videos per week are more likely to have multiple sex partners and to be diagnosed with a sexually transmitted disease.[37]

» Reports of molestation of very young children are increasing. More than one-third of all child victims may be five years old or younger; children as young as one week old have been molested.[38]

» "Marketing Sex to Children," from the Campaign for a Commercial-Free Childhood, showed that children are bombarded with sexual content and messages.[39]

» Before parents raised an outcry, Abercrombie & Fitch marketed a line of thong underwear decorated with sexually provocative phrases such as "Wink Wink" and "Eye Candy" to ten-year-olds.[40]

NOTES

Chapter 3: Noodles and Boxes

1. Bill and Pam Farrel, *Men Are Like Waffles—Women Are Like Spaghetti* (Eugene, OR: Harvest House, 2001).

Chapter 4: Mirror, Mirror

1. Michael Strober and Meg Schneider, *Just a Little Too Thin: How to Pull Your Child Back from the Brink of an Eating Disorder* (Cambridge, MA: Da Capo, 2005).
2. Carol Emery Normandi and Laurelee Roark, *Over It: A Teen's Guide to Getting Beyond Obsessions with Food and Weight* (Novato, CA: New World Library, 2001).
3. Margo Maine and Joe Kelly, *The Body Myth: Adult Women and the Pressure to Be Perfect* (Hoboken, NJ: Wiley & Sons, 2005).
4. Center for Consumer Freedom, *An Epic of Obesity Myths*, 2005.
5. Kaiser Family Foundation, "Sexual Health of Adolescents and Young Adults in the United States," January 2011, http://www.kff.org/womenshealth/upload/3040-05.pdf.
6. Center for Consumer Freedom, *An Epic of Obesity Myths*.
7. Farrel, *Men Are Like Waffles*.
8. H. Weinstock, S. Berman, and W. Cates, "Sexually Transmitted Diseases Among American Youth: Incidence and Prevalence Estimates, 2000," *Perspectives on Sexual and Reproductive Health* 36, no. 6 (2004), 10.
9. Strober and Schneider, *Just a Little Too Thin*.

Chapter 7: Who's Your Daddy?

1. John Eldredge, *Wild at Heart* (Nashville: Thomas Nelson, 2001).

Chapter 8: Five Questions Girls Ask (And How to Answer Them)

1. Farrel, *Men Are Like Waffles*.

Chapter 9: What Guys Don't Say

1. Leah Ariniello, "Gender and the Brain," Society for Neuroscience, http://web.sfn.org/content/Publications/BrainBriefings/gender.brain.html.

2. Lillian Glass, *He Says, She Says* (New York: Pedigree, 1993).
3. Nancy Ammon Jianakoplos and Alexander Bernasek, "Are Women More Risk Averse?" *Economic Injury* 36, no. 4 (October 1998), 620–30.
4. Sheila Brownlow, Rebecca Whitener, and Janet M. Rupert, "'I'll Take Gender Differences for $1000!' Domain-Specific Intellectual: Success on Jeopardy," *Sex Roles* (February 1998).

Chapter 11: Guys and Commitment

1. Donald Miller, *Searching for God Knows What* (Nashville: Thomas Nelson, 2004).
2. *Merriam-Webster Online Dictionary*, 2006, s.v. "commitment," http://www.m-w.com/dictionary/commitment (definition 2).

Chapter 13: Guys Have Secrets

1. Justin Lookadoo and Hayley Dimarco, *The Dateable Rules: A Guide to the Sexes* (Grand Rapids: Revell, 2004).

Chapter 14: Dating Advice from Guys

1. Robert E. Rector, et al., "The Harmful Effects of Early Sexual Activity and Multiple Sexual Partners Among Women: A Book of Charts," The Heritage Foundation, 26 June 2003.

Chapter 17: That Sex Stuff

1. Centers for Disease Control and Prevention, National Center for Health Statistics, Division of Vital Statistics, various years, http://www.cdc.gov/.
2. Ibid.
3. Centers for Disease Control and Prevention, Sexually Transmitted Disease Surveillance, 2004 (Atlanta: U.S. Department of Health and Human Services, 2005).
4. Centers for Disease Control and Prevention, National Center for Health Statistics, Division of Vital Statistics, various years.
5. Ibid.
6. Rector, et al., "The Harmful Effects of Early Sexual Activity."
7. Robin Warshaw, *I Never Called It Rape: The Ms. Report on Recognizing, Fighting and Surviving Date and Acquaintance Rape* (New York: Harper Perennial, 1994). United States Department of Justice, Office of the Justice Programs, Bureau of Journal Statistics, "Criminal Victimization in the United States—Statistical Tables Index," http://www.ojp.usdoj.gov/bjs/abstract/cvus/rape_sexual_assault.htm.

8. Centers for Disease Control and Prevention, "Out-of-Wedlock Births Have Risen to a Third of All Births," National Center for Health Statistics, Division of Vital Statistics, various years.

9. Centers for Disease Control and Prevention, National Center for Health Statistics, Division of Vital Statistics, various years.

10. National Campaign to Prevent Teen Pregnancy, 1997. *Whatever Happened to Childhood? The Problem of Teen Pregnancy in the United States.* Washington, D.C.

11. Brownlow, et al., "'I'll Take Gender Differences for $1000!' Domain-Specific Intellectual: Success on Jeopardy."

12. N. Berglas, C. Brindis, and J. Cohen, *Adolescent Pregnancy and Childbearing in California* (PDF; Outside Source), California State Library Foundation, June 2003.

13. Centers for Disease Control and Prevention, "Out-of-Wedlock Births Have Risen to a Third of All Births."

14. Berglas, Brindis, and Cohen, *Adolescent Pregnancy and Childbearing in California.*

15. The Alan Guttmacher Institute, http://guttmacher.org/.

Chapter 20: Pressure

1. Steven B. Sample, *The Contrarian's Guide to Leadership* (San Francisco: Jossey-Bass, 2002).

Chapter 21: Seriously? You Have More Questions?

1. Warshaw, *I Never Called It Rape.* United States Department of Justice, Office of the Justice Programs, Bureau of Journal Statistics, "Criminal Victimization in the United States."

Chapter 23: True but Slightly Un-Awesome Things

1. The Alan Guttmacher Institute, http://guttmacher.org/.

2. M. L. Munson and P. D. Sutton, "Births, Marriages, Divorces, and Deaths: Provisional Data for 2004," *National Vital Statistics Reports* 53, no. 21 (2005).

3. National Campaign to Prevent Teen Pregnancy, "Fact Sheet: How Is the 34% Statistic Calculated?" quoted in S. K. Henshaw, *U.S. Teenage Pregnancy Statistics with Comparative Statistics for Women Ages 20–24* (New York: Alan Guttmacher Institute, 2004).

4. R. A. Maynard, ed., *Kids Having Kids: A Robin Hood Foundation Special Report on the Costs of Adolescent Childbearing* (New York: Robin Hood Foundation, 1996).

5. National Campaign to Prevent Teen Pregnancy, *Whatever Happened to Childhood?*

6. Ibid.

7. Centers for Disease Control and Prevention, National Center for Health Statistics, Division of Vital Statistics, various years.

8. Ibid.

9. Ibid.

10. Ibid.

11. Ibid.

12. Ibid.

13. Ibid.

14. Rector, et al., "The Harmful Effects of Early Sexual Activity."

15. Denise Holfers, et al., "Adolescent Depression and Suicide Risk: Association with Sex and Drug Behavior," *American Journal of Preventive Medicine* 27, no. 3 (2004).

16. Ibid.

17. Warshaw, *I Never Called It Rape.*

18. The National Center on Addiction and Substance Abuse at Columbia University (CASA).

19. Ibid.

20. Ibid.

21. D. G. Curtis, *Perspectives on Acquaintance Rape,* The American Academy of Experts in Traumatic Stress, http://www.aaets.org/arts/art13.htm/.

22. United States Department of Justice, Office of the Justice Programs, Bureau of Journal Statistics, "Criminal Victimization in the United States."

23. Ibid.

24. Ibid.

25. Curtis, *Perspectives on Acquaintance Rape.*

26. Rector, et. al, "The Harmful Effects of Early Sexual Activity."

27. United States Department of Justice, Office of the Justice Programs, Bureau of Journal Statistics, "Criminal Victimization in the United States."

28. United States Department of Justice, Coordinating Council on Juvenile Justice and Delinquency, Prevention Action Plan Update (October 2001).

29. United States Department of Justice, Office of the Justice Programs, Bureau of Journal Statistics, "Criminal Victimization in the United States."

30. Ibid.

31. Rector, et. al. "The Harmful Effects of Early Sexual Activity."

32. United States Department of Justice, Office of the Justice Programs, Bureau of Journal Statistics, "Criminal Victimization in the United States."

33. United States Department of Justice, Prevention Action Plan Update.

34. Curtis, *Perspectives on Acquaintance Rape*.

35. Centers for Disease Control and Prevention, National Center for Health Statistics, Division of Vital Statistics, various years.

36. National Victim Center and Crime Victims Research and Treatment Center, Rape in America: A Report to the Nation, 1992.

37. Centers for Disease Control and Prevention, National Center for Health Statistics, Division of Vital Statistics, various years.

38. United States Department of Justice, Office of the Justice Programs, Bureau of Journal Statistics, "Criminal Victimization in the United States."

39. Campaign for a Commercial-Free Childhood, "Marketing Sex to Children," http://www.commercialfreechildhood.org/factsheets /ccfc-facts%20marketingsex.pdf/.

40. Rector, et. al. "The Harmful Effects of Early Sexual Activity."